Using New Testament Greek in Ministry

A Practical Guide for Students and Pastors

David Alan Black

BAKER BOOK HOUSE
Grand Rapids, Michigan 49516

Published by Baker Books
a division of Baker Book House Company
P.O. Box 6287, Grand Rapids, MI 49516-6287

Third printing, September 1995

Printed in the United States of America

Library of Congress Cataloging-in-Publication Data

Black, David Alan, 1952–
    Using New Testament Greek in ministry : a practical guide for students and pastors / David Alan Black.
        p. cm.
    Includes bibliographical references and index.
    ISBN 0-8010-1043-8
    1. Bible. N.T. Greek—Versions. 2. Bible. N.T.—Homiletical use. 3. Greek language, Biblical. I. Title.
    BS1938.B49
    225.4′8—dc20   92–42175

ß HARGROVE

Using New Testament Greek in Ministry

In Gratitude

to the schools that during seventeen years
have allowed me to prepare preachers of the Gospel:

Talbot School of Theology in La Mirada, California

Grace Theological Seminary in Winona Lake, Indiana, and
(formerly in) Long Beach, California

Simon Greenleaf University in Anaheim, California

Bibelschule Walzenhausen in Walzenhausen, Switzerland

Freie Hochschule für Mission in Korntal, Germany

Contents

Preface and Acknowledgments

I have written this book for all who want to improve their skills in preparing messages from the New Testament. I hope it will find a ready response among busy pastors and pastors-in-the-making. My primary concern has been to motivate expositors to use their knowledge of Greek in ways that will glorify God. Just as importantly, as one who regularly preaches from the New Testament, I desire to see revival and renewal in the church. For the church—not the seminary—is God's number one priority in the world. If believers are to grow and to develop into mature believers and effectively functioning Christians, then it is of the utmost importance that pastors and other church leaders provide Bible-centered messages for their people. In what follows, I have tried to explain simply and clearly how a knowledge of Greek can play a meaningful role in that process.

Let us not underestimate the importance of our task. Paul once wrote to Timothy, "Be diligent to present yourself approved to God as a workman who does not need to be ashamed, handling accurately the word of truth" (2 Tim. 2:15 NASB). The same diligence required of Timothy is also required of preachers today. The Word of God must be handled accurately— or not handled at all.

If you have had at least one year of Greek but rarely (if ever) use your knowledge of the language in ministry, this book is for you. If you are currently learning Greek, this book can help you see the relevance of what you are studying. Whether pastor or student, my prayer is that you will strive to be a true student of God's Word and that *Using New Testament Greek in Ministry* will help you become an even more skillful one.

I wish to express my sincere appreciation to the following persons who helped make this book possible: Allan Fisher and Jim Weaver of Baker Book House, who believed in this project from the very beginning; David Aiken, who superbly edited the manuscript and also compiled the bibliography; the library staff of Biola University, who assisted my research in countless ways; Father Anselm and the religious community of the Prince of Peace Abbey, who gave me access to their library along with several days of solitude for reflection and writing; my prayer partners Mike Adams and Mike Quarry, who shared the burden of this book with me in prayer; my congregation at Granada Heights Friends Church, who allow me to use my creative abilities in the service of Christ; my wife Becky and my sons Nathan Alan and Matthew David, who provide a loving environment in which to live and work; and my Greek students, who bring me more joy than they will ever know.

Abbreviations

AV   Authorized Version

BAGD   *A Greek-English Lexicon of the New Testament and Other Early Christian Literature*, by Walter Bauer, William F. Arndt, F. Wilbur Gingrich, and Frederick W. Danker

BDF   *A Greek Grammar of the New Testament and Other Early Christian Literature*, by Friedrich Blass, Albert Debrunner, and Robert W. Funk

GNT   *The Greek New Testament*, edited by Kurt Aland, Matthew Black, Carlo M. Martini, Bruce M. Metzger, and Allen Wikgren

ISBE   *The International Standard Bible Encyclopedia*, edited by Geoffrey W. Bromiley

JB   Jerusalem Bible

KJV   King James Version

LB   Living Bible

LXX   Septuagint

NASB   New American Standard Bible

NEB   New English Bible

NIDNTT   *The New International Dictionary of New Testament Theology*, edited by Colin Brown

NIV   New International Version

NRSV   New Revised Standard Version

RSV   Revised Standard Version

TDNT   *Theological Dictionary of the New Testament*, edited by Gerhard Kittel and Gerhard Friedrich

TEV   Today's English Version

1

You and Your Greek New Testament

Clarifying Objectives

Why This Book?

They endure endless hours of lectures, stuff their minds with vocabulary, glut their bookshelves with expensive volumes, writhe over term papers, and agonize through scores of examinations. Greek students are a determined lot indeed. Even the most insensitive observer would sympathize with their plight. But when all the assignments are completed and the degrees bestowed, what will become of all this scholarship? Will the hideous chasm between the study desk and the pulpit be bridged? Or will the mysterious process of forgetting run its inevitable course?

To the pastor or ministerial student who has successfully negotiated a year or two of Greek, these questions are anything but theoretical. The trauma of transforming studies into sermons confronts most, if not all, young ministers. Walter Kaiser has gone so far as to speak of a "current crisis" in exegetical methodology. That crisis is the gap "between the steps generally outlined in most seminary or Biblical training classes in exegesis and the hard realities most pastors face every week as they prepare sermons."[1]

The problem is not that no one can say what a pastor should do; almost everyone can—and does. Both denominational leaders and congregational members expect the person who is preparing for ministry to be able to deliver messages from the New Testament that are based on careful exegesis of the original Greek. Yet a common complaint among pastors is that seminaries have done little to actually give guidance in exegesis once the student leaves the classroom. They ask for more help in knowing how to use Greek to increase their effectiveness as preachers and teachers.

This is, I am convinced, an accurate assessment and a legitimate request. In reviewing the substantial body of Greek literature produced over the past several decades, I have become disturbed at the scarcity of books that discuss how and why a knowledge of New Testament Greek can increase ministerial effectiveness. Strong facility in the biblical languages is regularly affirmed as a positive factor in ministry, but a practical and up-to-date manual that would help the young (and the not-so-young!) pastor formulate a realistic strategy for using Greek in ministry is yet lacking.

That is precisely why I have written this book. Its entire purpose is to prepare you to use Greek in your ministry. You may approach its contents in any way you wish, depending on your needs or desires. Do you want a quick overview of Greek exegesis? Scan chapter 3, "Getting Oriented," for it is designed to be your basic guide to New Testament interpretation based on the original Greek. Do you want help on buying the best Greek tools for your personal

1. Walter C. Kaiser Jr., *Toward an Exegetical Theology: Biblical Exegesis for Preaching and Teaching* (Grand Rapids: Baker, 1981), p. 18.

library? Turn to chapter 2, "Off the Shelf and into Yourself," and I am confident you will find the information you are seeking. Are you curious about the proper steps in doing a word study? In chapter 4, "Developing Your Exegetical Skills," you will find fundamental guidelines on deciphering these basic building blocks of language. Do you need to know how to move from text to sermon? Or analyze syntax? Or diagram a passage in Greek? Or do you want to know how the personal computer can help you in your study of Scripture? Drawing from many years of experience in teaching New Testament Greek, I have tried to give you the fundamentals in each area.

Of course, all I—or anyone else—can give you in a book about the practical use of Greek, no matter what its size or how great its goals, are the basic facts, the most accurate guidelines available, an informed selection of subjects, and, in my case, a bias in favor of practicality (over mere theory). You must translate all of this into whatever is right for you. In chapter 4, for example, you will find straightforward rules for analyzing the structure of any Greek text. But you must decide how often you will use this technique when you prepare your sermons. In the same chapter you will find help on resolving textual problems in your chosen passage. But you must determine when it is practical for you to follow this advice. All of us must decide for ourselves what and how much information about Greek we will use in our personal lives and ministries.

Of course, you probably would not be reading this book unless you were already convinced that a knowledge of New Testament Greek is of some practical value. Somewhere along the way you discovered the excitement and rewards of studying the New Testament in its original language. The pitfall is that even our best intentions can be weakened by distractions and moods. Therefore, before we look at some basic guidelines for using Greek in ministry, it may be a good idea to review some of the major reasons for studying Greek in the first place.

Why Study Greek?

It was a preacher named Martin Luther who said, "Let us zealously hold to the [biblical] languages. . . . The languages are the sheath in which this sword of the Spirit is contained."[2] It is no accident that this tribute to the biblical languages comes from an acknowledged prince of evangelical Christianity and out of the heart of the Protestant Reformation, which was Germany's version of America's Great Awakening. Facility in the biblical languages has long been recognized as a basic requirement for pastoral ministry. No person is likely to grasp the intended meaning of the Bible, on its deepest level, unless that person learns to read and, in some sense, think in Hebrew and Greek.

Oddly, however, while there is general agreement that the biblical languages are essential for an effective preaching ministry, there is much less agreement on the place of the languages in the seminary curriculum. For example, a report by the American Association of Theological Schools documented a notable decline in the study of the biblical languages in our nation's theological institutions. The report lamented, "Even in those schools where the languages are still required, the amount of requirement has frequently been reduced from what used to obtain when theological and classical learning were so closely held together."[3] The study went on to indicate that most ministerial students have scarcely begun to explore the hidden wealth of the biblical text. They have settled for a comparatively dull, dreary mediocrity.

2. In an essay entitled "To the Councilmen of All Cities in Germany That They Establish and Maintain Christian Schools," in *Luther's Works* (ed. Jaroslav Pelikan and Helmut T. Lehmann; Philadelphia: Muhlenberg, 1962), vol. 45, pp. 359–60.

3. H. Richard Niebuhr, Daniel D. Williams, and James M. Gustafson, *The Advancement of Theological Education* (New York: Harper, 1957), pp. 92–93.

Problems in Greek Instruction

This state of affairs did not spring up overnight, but is the result of multiple factors that have developed through many decades. Noting these factors here will help to identify certain issues that are fundamental to the general approach taken in this book.

In the first place, the present malaise of language instruction is at least partly attributable to the fact that the teaching of language tends to be dominated by *content* to the neglect of *understanding*. Traditional emphases in Greek instruction have been overly abstract, intellectual, even esoteric. Students sometimes feel the way church father Saint Augustine felt about his Greek teachers. "The drudgery of learning a foreign language," he complained, "sprinkled bitterness over all the sweetness of the Greek tales. I do not know a word of the language: and I was driven with threats and savage punishments to learn."[4] This statement is an exaggeration, of course; but I wonder how many seminarians could echo Augustine's sentiments.

In criticizing an overly intellectual approach to Greek, I am not, of course, questioning the need for studying the biblical languages. The student or pastor whose heart beats with passion for the Word of God is willing to endure the inevitable drudgery that comes with seemingly endless lists of words and forms. There comes a time, however, when all but the most devoted disciples of paradigms and principal parts ask, "What good is all this? How will this help us as pastors?" These questions are neither stupid nor smart-alecky. Too often Greek teachers try to turn their seminary courses into a repetition of their doctoral work, just as newly minted Hebrew instructors sometimes read their graduate seminar notes to their classes. Neither teacher has given enough thought to the needs and abilities of their students—they are trying too hard to make their courses intel-

4. *Confessions* §1:14.

lectually viable to themselves. And from this noxious root grows a multitude of poisonous plants that transform what should be a pleasant garden into a poison-laden wilderness.

This crisis in pedagogy stems largely from the alliance between seminaries and the scholarly academy. Seminary professors, trapped between the demands of scholarly publication and the values of the church, have generally opted to please the academy. The result is that seminaries have sometimes tolerated an approach to Greek instruction that reduces the New Testament to an object of scientific inquiry, relegates Greek to an academic exercise, and restricts the Greek New Testament to being a sourcebook of information with little or no regard for its life-changing power—all, of course, to the detriment of the local congregation.

Thankfully, this development is not irreversible. In fact, today there are indications that Greek teachers are more aware than ever of the need to reform their methodology, to make their materials relevant to ministerial students, and to redress the false dichotomy between academic preparation and practical training. It is not to impose but rather to challenge, stimulate, and inspire that the Greek instructor is asked to enter the classroom. In such a setting the teacher is free to become a helpmate and guide, and the student is free to look at language study as a practical means to a very practical end. Still, many educators agree that not enough is being done in our schools to relate training in the languages to "the work of the ministry" (Eph 4:12 NRSV). One may count on one's fingers the number of books that even attempt to bridge this gap between classroom and pulpit. It is abundantly clear today that Greek teachers need to recover their pedagogical bearings and restore vision and focus to their distinctive contribution to the enterprise of ministerial training.

Second, the present decline in language instruction may perhaps be said to stem from the enormous amount of material covered in the typical exegesis course. Like the Dutch boy with his finger in the dike, Greek students are terrified about the "whole wild sea" that is out there. Greek is the object of a lifetime's work, requiring even the specialist to work hard just to keep up with the new ideas that are constantly being advanced. If Greek is this challenging for scholars, it is not surprising that many seminarians are tempted to surrender quietly their budding interest in the language or else opt out of taking Greek altogether.

This is no easy problem to solve. Any sane educator agrees that the languages are a "good discipline," but the benefits of Hebrew and Greek are easily smothered in a mass of linguistic minutiae. Moreover, once the student enters the busy marketplace of life, the emphasis shifts dramatically from preparation to application. Only what is essential about the languages matters now, but even "the essentials" are difficult to define and even more difficult to retain. What is needed in this grammatical jungle is a road map—a presentation of the most basic tools and principles of exegesis in a form designed to encourage the actual use of Greek. A road map gives us a view of the situation as a whole at the same time that it directs us to areas we may wish to explore in detail for ourselves. A guide to Greek exegesis should serve the same functions, but the typical textbook is far too detailed to function in this way.

My third concern about Greek instruction is a corollary of the first two. The abstract and academic way in which many students learn Greek contributes little to what I consider to be the primary aim of a seminary education: to prepare expository preachers of God's Word. For too long, the mind (exegesis) and the heart (homiletics) have been prone to say to the other, "I have no need of you" (1 Cor 12:21 NRSV). Seminary professors often feel that their responsibility in teaching Greek ends with grammatical explanation. They apparently believe that somehow their students will bridge the gap between exegesis and homiletics. I have even known some teachers who deliberately avoided pointing out applications of Greek because, they reasoned, application follows automatically. What's more, few exegetical handbooks move to this stage of exegesis, even though application is the obvious culmination of the exegetical process, with the sermon as the ultimate goal.

How is it, one wonders, that a book given by God to transform lives seems so unproductive when taught in the very places where it is most honored and best known? The answer, at least partly, may lie in the absence of meaningful application. By "application" I am referring to the process of communicating the present-day relevance of the text, specifying how a knowledge of New Testament Greek may be translated into action and urging students to make that transference personally. The burden of a full-orbed philosophy of Greek instruction must be to show how students can discover and communicate the text's relevance in a specific way and how they can call for a response to that meaning. To exclude either of these elements—relevance and response—wrongly implies that Greek is incapable of contributing to one's personal and spiritual growth or to one's ministerial effectiveness.

A final factor in the present malaise of instruction in the biblical languages is undoubtedly the increasing tendency in education toward subjectivism. As Allan Bloom pointedly observes, "There is one thing a professor can be absolutely certain of: almost every student entering the university believes, or says he [or she] believes, that truth is relative."[5] Unfortunately, seminaries have not been immune to the deadening effect of this form of subjectivism. In many of our theological institutions there seems to be a subtle shift from a concern with the exposition of objective truth to a concern with the subjective applicability of truth. If truth is relative, why pursue it—especially if this means having to learn Hebrew and Greek to do so? One result of this type of thinking is that exegesis as a vital aspect of theological education is now sometimes eclipsed by skill-oriented pro-

5. Allan Bloom, *The Closing of the American Mind* (New York: Simon & Schuster, 1987), p. 25.

grams. As documented in the above-mentioned American Association of Theological Schools report, seminary curriculums over the past generation show a steady demise of the exegetical disciplines. This abandoning of the biblical languages and of courses in exegesis suggests that the study of the original languages may soon become a thing of the past in American theological education.

Principles of Greek Instruction

As I struggled with these concerns, I asked myself whether I had ever been guilty of committing any of these pedagogical "sins." The truth is that I have. To be honest, Dave Black speaking on educational theory is a little like Nero speaking on fire safety. But through the years I've learned to ask the question: "What practical motivations can I give to help students use their knowledge of Greek more effectively?" As I thought about this question, new insights and a fresh approach to New Testament Greek instruction were beginning to take place in my thinking. In time, I arrived at three basic conclusions.

First, I began to see that the primary purpose of instruction in Greek is service to Christ's body, the church. Training in New Testament Greek may be an exceedingly important part of the seminary curriculum, but it is primarily a servant's heart—a love for God and for God's people—that makes this activity worthwhile. I have found time and again that, wherever this heart of dedication to Christ and his people exists, preaching and other applications of Greek (and Hebrew) flow naturally. An old Scottish proverb puts it beautifully: "Greek, Hebrew, and Latin all have their proper place. But it is not at the head of the cross, where Pilate put them, but at the foot of the cross, in humble service to Christ." Put less imaginatively, the success of a seminary education is to be measured, not in terms of how much grammar and theology we have managed to cram into the heads of our students, but in terms of whether we have produced mature human beings who are dedicated to serving God and others to the very best of their ability.

This last statement is not meant to negate the need for biblical knowledge. The essence of effective preaching is the ability to simplify without becoming simplistic. This requires understanding on a deep and profound level. R. C. Sproul once observed that great preachers are like icebergs—they reveal on the surface only about ten percent of what is actually there in substance. Such depth is always based on an accurate and adequate knowledge of one's subject. But knowledge per se is neither the starting point nor the goal of seminary education. True education is rooted in a radical commitment to putting knowledge to good use. This may be a tough challenge, but it is the key to ministry in all its fullness. Settling for anything less only feeds the pride of those students who want degrees more than wisdom, and praise rather than equipment for service.

Second, I rediscovered that a knowledge of New Testament Greek is a potential source of spiritual renewal. I began to see that the aim of Greek instruction was much higher than the teaching of methods or the solving of exegetical problems. As important as these goals are, my main concern in teaching became the spiritual development of both minister and congregation.

This discovery that Greek is a potential source of spiritual power has been made more than once. As a student in Basel, Switzerland, I learned that when Erasmus published his Greek New Testament there in 1516, a great tumult spread over Europe. The outcry was loudest among those who led corrupt or spiritually apathetic lives. In his *Life and Letters of Erasmus*, J. A. Froude describes the spiritual earthquake produced when the Greek New Testament was allowed to shed its light:

> Never was [a] volume more passionately devoured. A hundred thousand copies were soon sold in France alone. The fire spread, as it spread behind Samson's foxes in the Philis-

tines' corn. The clergy's skins were tender from long impurity. They shrieked from pulpit and platform, and made Europe ring with their clamour.[6]

Many today are discovering that the God who spoke through Erasmus's Greek New Testament still speaks to sensitive hearts. Reading the original text is no mere recital of past events. Rather, it is a part of God's means of bringing us in touch with the power and effect of the text and applying its truths to our lives. Scripture that is imbued with this kind of power cannot be passively received. In other words, Greek does not exist for itself. It exists only as a tool for edification. If it is content to be confined to the halls of learning, it has lost its prophetic character, and with that its integrity.

Finally, I began to see that it was only out of this sense of personal devotion to Christ and this commitment to spiritual renewal in the church that Greek instruction made any sense. If our purpose as preachers is to understand and proclaim what God has said to his people for their spiritual growth, and if it pleased God to reveal himself in the Greek language, then a knowledge of New Testament Greek should not be regarded as a luxury, but as an imperative.

"But what about the accuracy and sufficiency of English translations?" I have been asked this question a thousand times, and my answer is always the same. For while it is certainly true that the Bible—in any language—is plain enough for the believer to understand what is sufficient for his or her practical needs, it is also true that persons who expend effort in the search for truth will be rewarded in accordance with their labors. The serious pastor, for whom the Bible is the most important book in the world, wants something more than an "average" understanding, especially if that pastor wants to be able to teach others its truths.

6. J. A. Froude, *Life and Letters of Erasmus* (New York: Scribner/London: Longmans, Green, 1894), p. 127.

It is precisely in this context of ministering to others the truth of God's Word that preachers most clearly see their need to understand the intricacies of Greek. Professionals should always be better informed than their clients. An automobile driver does not need to understand the complexities of internal combustion, but the mechanic does. The physician must be able to diagnose the patient's problem with far greater precision than the patient could. Is it, then, unreasonable for the church to expect expositors of Holy Scripture to derive practical help and illumination from the original text of Scripture?

Consider, for a moment, the alternative. Pastors who do not know Greek are forced to borrow their ideas from others. They are slaves to the commentators, but have no means to check their accuracy. The best tools of interpretation are beyond their reach. Not even the English translations they use are completely trustworthy. Worst of all, without thorough training in Greek they may discover that they are passing on in the name of God their own ignorance, based upon erroneous interpretations.

Let me repeat: I am not arguing for a knowledge of Greek per se. Greek must not be taught like Edmund Hillary's Mount Everest—"because it's there." But for that very reason it cannot be ignored. Greek is most certainly "there," and no preacher can be called an informed professional without an extensive knowledge of it.

Guidelines for Using Greek in Christian Nurture

Our goal, then, in studying Greek is to use our knowledge in the service of Christ and for the upbuilding of his body. It cannot be said too emphatically nor too often that the purpose of Greek exegesis is not merely to inform, but to persuade and to call forth an appropriate response to the God whose Word is being proclaimed. This response will consist of repentance, faith, obedience, love, zeal, and a hundred other virtues, but it will never consist of fallow knowledge. If this conviction draws criticism as being too narrow or applicational, I must endure it; but I cannot see that the New Testament will sanction any lower purpose for exegesis. The considerations that follow in this book will, I trust, make this clear.

But how are we to go about our task? Through much prayer and with the help of the Holy Spirit, of course. Yet the wise pastor is not averse to following some common-sense principles. At the risk of oversimplifying complex issues, let me suggest three guidelines to consider as you prepare to use Greek in ministry.

First, keep in mind that there are no painless methods for grasping the meaning of God's Word. Regardless of what some people may say, there is nothing magical about Greek exegesis. Exegetical aids can make our work simpler, but serious Bible study requires time and effort. Even with the illuminating ministry of the Holy Spirit the New Testament is tough reading, for in it God has communicated to us his infinite wisdom. Great minds have devoted a lifetime to its study, only to feel as though they were wading on the shore of a limitless ocean.

The great paradox of Christianity is, of course, that the Bible is an "open book" for anyone who takes it seriously. In fact, there is no real substitute for the benefits resulting from one's own hard work in the text. But these benefits do not emerge without a considerable amount of midwifery. We may never reach the heights of understanding attained by Bible scholars, but if we are diligent we will certainly reap results. The psalmist sensed this principle three millenniums ago (Ps. 126:6 NRSV):

> Those who go out weeping,
>   bearing the seed for sowing,
> shall come home with shouts of joy,
>   carrying their sheaves.

In the second place, we who preach from the New Testament must be keenly aware of the temptation of spiritual pride in using Greek in ministry. Probably the greatest danger in language study is for Greek to become centered on itself. Then, whether in the study or the pulpit, it subtly starts pushing itself, not Christ. It is distressing to see more and more of this kind of abuse of Greek among ministers. Instead of "holding forth the word of life" (Phil. 2:16), they are pushing themselves and their knowledge. Their pulpits become a place where the Bible is taught, but also where "the creature is worshiped rather than the Creator" (Rom. 1:25).

Because knowledge ministers so easily to pride (1 Cor. 8:1), I generally counsel students to leave Greek aside altogether when they enter the pulpit. The most gifted ministers of my acquaintance make it a rule to leave the dust and debris of exegesis in the workshop. They know that a great deal of damage can be done by persons who use Greek to "prove" something. Here we might learn a lesson from the cultists, who love to flaunt their "superior" knowledge of the Scriptures by appealing to the original languages to "prove" orthodox interpretations of the Bible wrong. The fact is that most cultists have only a superficial knowledge of Hebrew and Greek, if any at all. In contrast, responsible preaching recognizes that truth is never settled or proven one way or another on the basis of Greek words or grammar alone. The preacher who merely spouts off grammar, however brilliantly or forcefully, has completely missed this point.

But perhaps the greatest reason why technical jargon in preaching is so damaging is because it causes the expositor to lose sight of the main purpose of exegesis—to communicate the meaning of God's Word as clearly as possible. Preachers are regrettably prone to try and impress people with their profound exegetical abilities. The greater the education, the greater the danger. But the truth is that people aren't impressed with participles and prepositions. They are not even faintly interested in the aorist passive imperative. People want preaching anchored in their world, preaching that says: "Here is what the text says, and this is what it is calling us to do." Exegetes should never forget that the Greek New Testament was written in the common language of the day. Its appeal was to the people in the street, for it spoke clearly a language they understood.

And so it must be with us. It is essential that Jesus Christ be dynamically preeminent in our pulpits. To allow the knowledge of Greek to become too obvious is fleshly, even vulgar. Greek expert A. T. Robertson said it best: "No parade or display of learning is called for. Results and not processes suit the pulpit. The non-theological audience can usually tell when the sermon is the result of real work. The glow is still in the product."[7]

My final suggestion is a very practical one and is directed primarily to those of you who are now studying Greek. Your chances for successfully using New Testament Greek in ministry are greatly enhanced if you take charge of the learning situation. Setting realistic goals will help you to select the right language-learning program, if you have not already done so, or help clarify the benefits of the program you are already in. Unless the classroom objectives are filtered through your own personal objectives, they will remain simply lessons in a book, hours spent in class, and pages of written assignments that have no application to real life. Having objectives firmly in mind will also help you select the most suitable textbooks and helps. Finally, by setting realistic goals for yourself you can more easily sustain your motivation and interest.

To help us think of setting goals in language learning, let us examine the system in use by the Foreign Service Institute of the United States Department of State and by the Educational Testing Service, a publisher of standardized tests.

7. A. T. Robertson, *The Minister and His Greek New Testament* (New York: Doran, 1923; repr. Grand Rapids: Baker, 1977), pp. 82–83.

Depending on your desires and needs, you will want to aim for one of the following levels of proficiency. These levels are called R-levels (R for "reading").

R-1 (Elementary Proficiency). At the first level, a person can read only the simplest prose containing the most common words and grammatical constructions. Chances are the student will not be able to read material much more difficult than the translation assignments in an elementary textbook. Heavy reliance on a dictionary is normal. If this level will satisfy your needs as you define them, then mastering the Greek alphabet and learning to use some of the basic Greek study aids will probably help you more than taking additional courses in grammar. Certainly a serious layperson can achieve this level of proficiency.

R-2 (Limited Working Proficiency). At the second stage, a person can read uncomplicated but authentic prose that contains many common words and basic sentence patterns. Anything more difficult would mean frequent reliance on a dictionary. To achieve this level of proficiency, a student needs more grammar, more vocabulary, and greater effort than for R-1.

R-3 (Professional Proficiency). At the third level, a person can grasp the essentials of standard but uncomplicated prose without a dictionary. If you are aiming at this level, you should make sure that you familiarize yourself with the special vocabulary used in the New Testament. It is also a good idea to invest in a quality Greek lexicon at this time.

R-4 (Full Proficiency). At the final stage, a person can read anything in the foreign language without a dictionary. In order to attain this level of proficiency, one must read as much in the language as possible. A very large vocabulary is the key that unlocks the door to this level. As a rule, very few people—Greek teachers included—attain such a high level. But it is a goal to be aspired to if one is ambitious enough.

If you can identify the level you want to or need to achieve, you will be better able to focus your efforts. You will also feel more positive about your achievements be-cause they will become more evident to you. If your aspi-rations are really high and you want to be able to read New Testament Greek with a great deal of fluency and pre-cision of vocabulary, you will need several years of study. In general, however, the R-2 level of proficiency is a real-istic goal for anyone who has had at least one year of in-struction in New Testament Greek. If this level is your goal, you should make sure that your training in the lan-guage includes enough grammar and vocabulary for you to be able to translate the New Testament with the help of a good lexicon.

The Path Ahead

Ironic as it may sound, the conclusion reached in this chapter is that a knowledge of Greek can significantly en-hance your God-given ministry. I have written this book to inspire you to use Greek in a way that will glorify God and edify his people. But what are *you* looking for as you read this book? How will it fit your expectations? What will you find here?

In our next chapter we will look at the most important study aids designed to assist you in moving from text to ser-mon. No matter how much you will be able to do your own study of the original text, you will still need the advice of seasoned guides who can lead you through troublesome terrain and keep you from getting lost. For the most part, you can move from text to sermon with a minimum amount of outside help, provided that help is of the highest quality. For those just starting out, chapter 2 recommends a basic library containing a minimum number of books need-ed to use Greek in ministry. It also covers books that are not essential but are nevertheless important.

Chapters 3 and 4 attempt to apply basic hermeneutical principles in an effort to develop a practical approach to New Testament exegesis. As expositors of God's Word, our

task is to go from the "there" of the ancient biblical world to
the "here" of the modern world. Our dual concern is with
"what God said" and "what God is telling us today." Preaching is simply an attempt to "fuse" these two worlds. Of
course, getting the Word from Palestine to Peoria, from
Jerusalem to Jersey, is not an easy task. Like Jacob of old,
the preacher of today must be willing to enter a wrestling
match with the text before it gives up its blessing. Accord-
ingly, we will present some basic rules and guidelines for
Greek exegesis and show how to apply these in moving
from the biblical scene to the contemporary one. We will
consider three basic questions of interpretation: Where do
we find our passage? What did our passage convey to its
first readers? How does our passage apply to contemporary
life? This section, developing a framework for historical,
grammatical, and theological interpretation, is the heart of
the book, showing how the biblical text constitutes the basis
for application to modern living.

Finally, chapter 5 offers an opportunity for you to apply
the principles of this book to a specific New Testament passage. Of course, no book can actually provide that experience for its readers, but the present one endeavors to
simulate it by setting forth an actual example of Greek exegesis. As you work through this passage, you are encouraged to use and adapt the model of exegesis found in this
book. The central task at this point is to help you to secure
the experience, to engage in the work, to take the journey!

I could add more details about this volume, but I'm sure
you've got the idea. Before we get started, however, allow
me a few final exhortations.

First, relax. Anxiety about being able to comprehend this
or that detail can make any reader functionally blind. Instead, try to enjoy the book, put it aside for a while if you
become bored or confused, and leave your brain to take
care of the rest.

Second, do not try to memorize anything you read in this
book. The effort to memorize is frequently destructive of

comprehension. On the contrary, with comprehension the process of memorization will take care of itself. Your mind has had longer experience than you can recall in remembering what is really important.

Finally, do not give up! An apple seed may lie dormant for years, but surround it with warm soil and the right amount of moisture, and it sprouts. So be persistent! If you are, your reward will be the privilege of reveling in the riches of the greatest literary treasure of all time. "Jesus shines in the pages of the Greek New Testament," wrote A. T. Robertson. "He shines there still for all who will take the trouble to see. He is the Light of the World. No obscurantist can hide that Light. No one can afford to neglect that Light. The Greek New Testament is still the Torchbearer of Light and Progress for the world."[8]

Stop and Think

Why are you taking (or have you taken) New Testament Greek? Are you sufficiently motivated to use your knowledge of the language in ministry (why or why not)? Which level of reading proficiency are you aiming for?

8. Ibid., p. 116.

2

Off the Shelf
and into Yourself

Selecting the Right Tools for Greek Exegesis

In this electronic age, it may well be that a good library is the last thing expected of a pastor. For years the doomsayers have been prophesying the demise of the book as a learning tool. Let the prognosticators say what they will, but I don't think the book is a dinosaur, any more than I think writers are going to stop writing. It is ironic that at the height of the computer's popularity, more people than ever are buying and reading books. With all its flaws and shortcomings, the codex is here to stay.

Few of us could contemplate a world without books. Hugh Martin emphasizes this point in introducing his classic work *Great Christian Books*: "The influence of books can scarcely be exaggerated. In the long run the writer is more powerful than the soldier; it is the thinker who recruits and moves the army."[1] One need think only of a Hegel or a Marx to see that Martin is right. In the Christian world,

1. Hugh Martin, *Great Christian Books* (Philadelphia: Westminster, 1946), p. 9.

books like Saint Augustine's *Confessions* or Bunyan's *Pilgrim's Progress* have had no less influence.

If there is a thinker behind every great movement, there is a library behind every great preacher. What tools are to mechanics, books are to preachers. Just as no mechanic can do an effective job without adequate tools to perform precision work, so no pastor can ever hope to expound the Bible without good books. It is the height of folly for any pastor to attempt to preach God's Word without proper exegetical and expository tools. We are never so competent in our knowledge of the Scriptures that we can afford to despise the helps provided by the great minds of the past and the present.

The purpose of this chapter is to offer guidance in the selection and use of books that can help you use Greek both to understand and to communicate the meaning of the New Testament more effectively. My task has been simplified by the numerous guides to New Testament study aids already available. The most helpful resources are David M. Scholer's *Basic Bibliographical Guide for New Testament Exegesis*, Ralph P. Martin's *New Testament Books for Pastor and Teacher*, and Erasmus Hort's *Bible Book: Resources for Reading the New Testament*. These books might well be read alongside the present one, in particular the practical tips by Hort on how and where to buy books. Like these scholars, I propose to magnify and glorify the reading of books, not because as a Greek professor I think I ought to (though indeed I ought to), but because intelligent reading is of the very essence of responsible exegesis and because failure to consult these tools immeasurably impoverishes both preacher and congregation. In fact, there is now such an abundance of exegetical helps available that the pastor who ignores them cannot avoid the charge of superficiality and neglect.

Naturally a brief chapter such as this one must have certain limitations. On the one hand, I have opted to present a discriminating list of books rather than an exhaustive inventory. My purpose is to help you forge a path through the endlessly growing jungle of books on the New Testament. On the other hand, the works cited here are given fuller annotations than you will find in most bibliographies. I hope that what I have written will be a helpful guide in understanding these books, though I make no pretense of having said anything that will be new to frequent users of these tools. My aim, very simply, has been to offer recommendations of books that in my experience deserve first place on the pastor's bookshelf. These resources are expensive and represent a sizable investment—but an investment made only once and for a lifetime.

On the Use of Reference Tools

Before looking at these helps, however, perhaps a few preliminary remarks about the use of study tools are in order.

First, keep in mind that not all Greek helps serve the same purpose or are intended for the same readership. Some books are standard reference works of scholarship, while others are specific resource tools. Many require no more than a passing familiarity with New Testament Greek. Hort, with just a tinge of sarcasm, characterizes the latter type of tool as "quick Greek." My own view is considerably less cynical. The busy pastor, frantically returning phone calls and racing to the hospital, should never hesitate to use any "crib" necessary to get at the languages. The dictum here is, "Halitosis is better than no breath at all," as one preacher has put it. Interlinears, parsing guides, analytical lexicons, or any other aid can and should be used without guilt or apology. Naturally, great care should be exercised to see that one's personal library is first equipped with the essential tools in the various areas of ministerial studies. Only when you have established a good basic library, including the best tools for Greek exegesis, can you afford to specialize.

Second, I have avoided listing those so-called helps that most scholars would consider truly useless and even dangerous. These books do not even merit the tag "quick

Greek." Such books may appeal to the curious and unin-
formed layperson, but they are worse than useless. They are
harmful and will hurt both preacher and congregation.
(These books shall, of course, remain nameless.)

Third, I would emphasize that reading has many advantages for your personal growth in Christ. It is chiefly in the
pastor's study that the individual minister is most likely to
grow as a student of Scripture, a servant of God, and a
preacher. Like a candle under a bushel, the excitement born
of continual preparation for expository preaching cannot be
hidden. This is not to say that the reading of good books will
make us better people overnight. Yet exegetical study serves
that purpose in bringing us under the influence of God's
Word and the Spirit through whom that Word comes to us.
Hence exegesis can be viewed, not merely as preparation
for preaching, but as preparation for life. It is actually feed-
ing on God's Word and having one's soul strengthened in
the process.

Finally, it should never be forgotten that, as valuable as
Greek tools are, they are a servant to and not a substitute
for the reading of the text itself. Even with the results of expert learning within easy reach, there is a peculiar freshness
in reading the very language employed by a Peter or a Paul
until, like the carcass of Samson's lion, it yields its meat and
sweetness. It is not enough to read about the New Testament; we must read the New Testament itself. In fact, study
aids are most helpful when they set us pondering the text
for ourselves, enabling it to grow in the soil of our souls and
become our own.

Ten Essential Tools

What, then, are the basic tools necessary to use Greek in
ministry? Let me recommend ten primary resources for
your personal library. Though I have acquired hundreds of
books during my career as a teacher and preacher, I find
myself going back to these ten tools over and over again. I

have recommended them to many pastors, and am confident that you will find them helpful—if you use them. (See the bibliography for full publication data of the reference works discussed in this chapter.)

1. An English Bible

In one sense, of course, the Bible is not a tool; it is what we are studying. However, we will consider the choice of a Bible along with the other tools, since an English version is simply an attempt to render accurately the meaning of the original languages.

Which version of the Bible should you use for serious study? The answer is: one version *and* other versions.

One version. This version should be the Bible you use regularly in personal study and preaching. For ease of memorization, it should be one of the major English translations such as the King James Version, the New American Standard Bible, the New International Version, or the New Revised Standard Version. If you have not already decided on a translation, let me remind you that (a) there is no perfect translation—each version has its own strengths and weaknesses; (b) among the major versions there is no completely unreliable translation; (c) versions produced by committees deserve special consideration, since they tend to be less idiosyncratic than translations produced by individuals; and (d) if you decide on using a literal translation for study, this version should be supplemented by at least one idiomatic translation.

Other versions. But the best way to use the wealth of translations available today is to purchase an edition that offers several translations in one. A comparative version allows for quick reference and easy comparison among the most widely used Bibles today.

One such edition is *The Bible from Twenty-six Translations*, edited by Curtis Vaughan. Instead of placing the versions side by side, Vaughan took the King James Version as the base text and noted every major departure from its wording in the American Standard Version, Revised Standard Version, New American Standard Bible, New English Bible, Berkeley, Moffatt, Phillips, Knox, Goodspeed, Living Bible, Amplified Bible, Basic English New Testament, Weymouth, Twentieth Century New Testament, plus the translations of Lamsa, Conybeare (only on Paul's Epistles), Alford, Broadus, Williams, and several others. These versions serve as a commentary on the text of the King James Version.

The best buy in my view, however, is *The Eight Translation New Testament*, which offers the entire New Testament in eight columns to the double page according to the King James Version, Living Bible, Phillips, Revised Standard Version, Today's English Version, New International Version, Jerusalem Bible, and New English Bible. No other volume contains so many important contemporary versions side by side. While it would be both impossible and needless to give a full description of all these versions here, it might be helpful to briefly highlight the various translations included in this volume.

King James Version (1611). The King James Version (KJV) of the Bible (also known as the Authorized Version [AV]) is by far the most widely circulated translation in English, and the exegete who does not use it regularly would do well to have it available. This version was produced in England between 1604 and 1611 by a group of Church of England scholars. Using the best resources available to them at the time, these scholars achieved a grandeur of style still admired today. The underlying Greek text of the New Testament is, however, based on manuscripts generally considered to be inferior to those discovered since the time of King James. These newer texts omit such passages as the conclusion of Mark's Gospel (Mark 16:9–20) and the story in the Gospel of John of the woman taken in adultery (John 7:53–8:11). Nevertheless, in its various editions the KJV is still widely used among Protestants. English professors often use it more than theologians because of its literary qualities, although much of its language has now become archaic.

Living Bible (1971). Conservative in orientation, the Living Bible (LB) is a paraphrase rather than a word-for-word translation. In fact, it is such a free rendering that in most places it is highly interpretive. Although the editors checked the work against the Greek and Hebrew, for the most part the LB is the KJV in modern clothing. The LB has often been called a paradox, since it is most popular among those whose view of Scripture might otherwise preclude paraphrasing it. Apparently there is no strong feeling that fidelity to Scripture is violated when the text is paraphrased rather than translated.

Phillips (1958). J. B. Phillips, a British pastor, sought to produce a version in contemporary English. The result was a translation that is considered to be one of the most successful of the modern translations by a single scholar. Its style is thoroughly idiomatic and often striking. For example, Phillips's translation of 1 Corinthians 8:2 reads: "For whatever a man may know, he still has a lot to learn." Here is another: "I am no shadowboxer; I really fight!" (1 Cor. 9:26b). Many are acquainted with the rendering of Romans 12:2a: "Don't let the world around you squeeze you into its own mold." Even though it is a free translation, Phillips deserves the preacher's attention.

Revised Standard Version (1952). The Revised Standard Version (RSV) sought to combine the accuracy of the English and American revised versions of 1881 and 1901, the literary quality of the KJV, and the style and idiom of contemporary English. It was designed for use in public worship as well as private study. While some have strongly criticized the RSV, much of this opposition has been based on misinformation and ignorance. For example, the RSV has been accused of denying the deity of Christ because it has the centurion at the cross saying that Jesus was "a son of God" (Mark 15:39) instead of "the Son of God." However, the parallel in Luke records the centurion as saying, "Certainly this was a righteous man" (Luke 23:47), which is hardly an ascription of deity. On the other hand, the deity of Christ is affirmed by the RSV in Titus 2:13: "Our great God and Savior Jesus Christ." Hence the RSV, like most translations, can be helpfully used, and is, in fact, probably the most widely read revision of the KJV in the world today.

Today's English Version (1966). Today's English Version (TEV) is a contemporary English New Testament translation prepared by Robert G. Bratcher and published by the American Bible Society in 1966. The whole Bible was subsequently published as the *Good News Bible* in 1976, although TEV remains the popular label. The TEV is intended both for those who speak English as their mother tongue and for those who speak it as an acquired language. It is widely used around the world, due mainly to the promotional work of the Bible societies.

New International Version (1978). The New International Version (NIV) was produced by over one hundred evangelical scholars under the sponsorship of the New York–based International Bible Society. It is an entirely new translation and not a revision of an older version. It is concerned with both accuracy of translation and readability. Its text is arranged in paragraph form with captions at the beginning of sections. For devotional reading, the NIV perhaps has no peer. Probably the main criticism that can be made against it is that it paraphrases too freely at times, and thus is less helpful for study purposes.

Jerusalem Bible (1966). Produced by the Dominican Biblical School in Jerusalem, the Jerusalem Bible (JB) is a new translation from the original Hebrew and Greek texts (rather than from the Vulgate). The English version is based on the original French translation. Archaic words have been eliminated, and terms such as *thee* and *thou* have been completely replaced by their modern equivalents. Thus the reader has a completely modern Bible translation in clear and dignified English.

New English Bible (1970). Planned and directed by the Church of Scotland (along with other church bodies in the United Kingdom), the New English Bible (NEB) is an entirely new translation and not a revision of the KJV. It is intended for both worship and study. The language is dignified and accurate, but many American readers have found it cumbersome.

One other modern version deserving of mention, though not included in *The Eight Translation New Testament,* is the New American Standard Bible (1971). Published by the Lockman Foundation of La Habra, California, the NASB is a revision of the American Standard Version of 1901. The New Testament, which appeared in 1963, utilizes the more recent Greek manuscripts and stays close to the original text. In fact, it is sometimes too prone to follow Greek word order or to reproduce too mechanically the wording or tenses of the original Greek. Nevertheless, the NASB is a solid translation made entirely by evangelical scholars. In addition, the RSV, the NEB, and the JB are now available in revised editions (the *New Revised Standard Version* [1989], the *Revised English Bible* [1989], and the *New Jerusalem Bible* [1985]). The NRSV is particularly commendable in light of its distinctive translation philosophy.[2]

What are the advantages in being able to consult so many versions of the New Testament? First and foremost, the various translations will show you how limited your understanding would be if you only had one version. Second, versions that provide a paragraph format will help you to identify complete units of thought, especially in complex theological books such as Romans or Hebrews. Third, a comparison of the various English translations will make you aware of possible textual variations in the underlying Greek text. For example, in 1 Corinthians 11:29 the KJV

---

2. See Bruce M. Metzger, "The New Revised Standard Version," in *Scribes and Scripture: New Testament Essays in Honor of J. Harold Greenlee,* edited by David Alan Black (Winona Lake, Ind.: Eisenbrauns, 1992), pp. 111–15.

reads "he that eateth and drinketh unworthily," while the
NIV has "anyone who eats and drinks." The problem of
whether or not the Greek word translated "unworthily" in
the KJV is original may prompt one to reassess the textual
evidence. Fourth, a glance at several versions may offset
any obscure renderings in the version you normally use for
preaching (e.g., in Rom. 12:20 the KJV's "coals of fire" is clar-
ified in the NIV's "burning coals"). Fifth, consulting several
versions will make you aware of important syntactical variations. For instance, a comparison of 2 Peter 1:1 in the KJV
("God and our Saviour Jesus Christ," referring to two persons) with the RSV ("our God and Savior Jesus Christ," referring to one person) alerts you to a syntactical problem
bearing on the deity of Christ. Sixth, some versions are
more consistent in their treatment of Greek words and their
English equivalents. For example, the noun κρίσις is translated by three different words in John 5 in the KJV ("judgment" [v. 22]; "condemnation" [v. 24]; and "damnation"
[v. 29]), while in the NASB the word is rendered uniformly
as "judgment," thus preserving the connection between the
three verses. Finally, having access to several versions will
alert you to the subtle nuances of the Greek vocabulary in
your passage and show you where a more in-depth word
study might be necessary. In Hebrews 1:1, for example, the
interpreter is exposed to several possible renderings of the
Greek adverbs πολυμερῶς and πολυτρόπως:

KJV	at sundry times and in divers manners
RSV	in many and various ways
NIV	at many times and in various ways
NEB	in fragmentary and varied fashion

It should be plain by now that English translations do not
absolve us of using the Greek text in exegesis. Since modern
versions disagree among themselves so frequently, as never
before the pastor needs a reliable basis for comparison. The

only adequate basis for this comparison is, of course, the original Greek text.

2. A Modern Edition of the Greek New Testament

Once you have selected the English passage to be expounded in your sermon, you will need to examine it in detail. It is at this point in the homiletical process that the original Greek becomes invaluable. Accuracy demands that we understand to the best of our ability the language underlying our modern translations of the New Testament.

When it comes to an up-to-date Greek New Testament, most scholars prefer to use the Nestle–Aland *Novum Testamentum Graece*, now in its twenty-sixth edition. Equally valuable is the third (corrected) edition of *The Greek New Testament*, edited by Kurt Aland, Matthew Black, Carlo M. Martini, Bruce M. Metzger, and Allen Wikgren (*GNT*). This volume contains the same text as the twenty-sixth edition of Nestle–Aland but has a more readable format. Although its critical apparatus cites fewer variants than the Nestle–Aland text, it does so with considerably fuller evidence. The editors explain in the preface that they deliberately confined the critical apparatus to variants of significance to translators. The editors have also provided evaluation markings to indicate the probability of the printed text in places of variation. The scale includes four grades: A (virtual certainty), B (some degree of doubt), C (a considerable degree of doubt), and D (a very high degree of doubt). With grades C and D, the reader ought to feel free to adopt a different reading than the one printed in the text. If one desires to know the rationale behind the editors' decisions, one can consult the committee's *Textual Commentary* (see #8 below).

All scholars of the New Testament have, of course, their own views on the probabilities of readings, and frequently the editors of the *GNT* have preferred readings rejected by other scholars. Nevertheless, the *GNT* is an indispensable tool and is deservedly the most popular Greek text in print.

Pastors will appreciate the fact that the text is divided by English section headings. In the Gospels these headings are followed by references to parallel passages.

3. An Exegetical Guide

Second only to the Greek New Testament is the need for a tool that will help the interpreter read the Greek text and produce a provisional translation. All we can desire is supplied by Fritz Rienecker's *Linguistic Key to the Greek New Testament*, translated and edited by Cleon L. Rogers Jr. For the work of rapid reading, nothing excels the *Linguistic Key*. Proceeding book by book through the entire New Testament, it provides parsing of verbs, basic definitions, and insights from the major grammars. Although the definitions are brief, enough information is provided to serve as a basis for a more detailed study. And although the book bypasses the more technical aspects of the text, it gives a good idea of the kinds of decisions interpreters face. On the negative side, readers may find it inaccurate in places (in Rom. 12:2, for example, the present imperative plus μή does not necessarily indicate the discontinuance of an action in progress); and occasionally it relies on dated views of lexicography (in Phil. 1:12, the noun προκοπή does not necessarily mean a "cutting forward"). But these are isolated examples, since on the whole the work is a monument to careful scholarship and sagacious judgment.

4. A Greek-English Lexicon

In addition to a basic guide to exegesis and translation, New Testament exposition requires a dictionary of Greek for probing the shades of meaning within individual words as well as the precise meanings of those words within a given passage. The standard lexicon for the Greek New Testament—and the one most frequently quoted in the commentaries—is Bauer, Arndt, Gingrich, and Danker's *Greek-English Lexicon of the New Testament and Other Early Christian Literature*, often abbreviated BAGD. The 1979 (second English) edition of this lexicon is based on the fifth German edition of 1958. The entries are arranged according to the Greek alphabet and include insights from recent papyri studies as well as references to later Christian writings, intertestamental literature, and inscriptions. The abundant bibliographical references to articles and books are of great assistance to pastors wishing to be well informed on past research. Frequent recourse to this dictionary will be particularly helpful when one is studying controversial terms (e.g., ἄνωθεν, αὐθεντέω, ἐπιούσιος, ἱστορέω). Even the smallest words such as prepositions and conjunctions are skillfully handled. But whatever one's reason for turning to a Greek-English lexicon, BAGD will be the first port of call. Its only possible weakness is that the forest is sometimes obscured by the trees.

A sixth edition of Bauer's German lexicon has recently been produced by the Institute for New Testament Textual Research in Münster. Over two hundred new entries and the rewriting of many of the original articles enhance the proven worth of the earlier editions. In fact, about one-third of the material in the sixth edition is new, including a great deal of material from both Christian and non-Christian writers. Among writers now cited for the first time are Justin Martyr, Irenaeus, Clement of Alexandria, and Origen. The additional material permits a comparative study of the "New Testament" vocabulary as it is used by writers later in the Christian tradition. There is also a notable increase in quotations from the Septuagint as well as from other Jewish literature in the Greek language. An English translation of this sixth edition is now being prepared.

Although Greek lexicons are versatile exegetical tools, it must be remembered that lexicographers themselves have often assumed the role of exegetes. This means that the data submitted by the lexicographer must always give way to exegesis. Nevertheless, a veritable feast awaits the preacher who seeks lexical help from BAGD. Consider, for example, the meaning of τράπεζα in Acts 6:2. Perhaps you have al-

ways assumed that the expression referred to serving
"tables," but a glance at BAGD reveals the very real possibility that the word is to be associated here with banking.
The implication is that the apostles were refusing the role of
bankers and not simply that of butlers. A similar example is
the word translated "inn" in Luke 2:7. A check of BAGD under κατάλυμα makes more lucid what the translators may
have obscured, since "guest room" is assigned to the only
other occurrence of this word in Luke's Gospel (22:11). The
fact that Luke used this word, rather than the technical
term for "inn" (πανδοχεῖον), suggests that a room had in fact
been reserved for Joseph and Mary but unfortunately was
overcrowded by the time they arrived.

5. A Greek Word Study Dictionary

If one wishes to go beyond BAGD and do individual word
studies, a dictionary of New Testament Greek terms is essential. Gerhard Kittel and Gerhard Friedrich's *Theological
Dictionary of the New Testament* (*TDNT*), translated and edited
by Geoffrey W. Bromiley, is regarded as the standard work
in the field. It contains nine volumes of lexical studies, plus
an index volume. (A one-volume abridgment of *TDNT* is
also available.) However, the articles in the earlier volumes
are somewhat out of date and the theological orientation
throughout is generally nonconservative. For these and
other reasons I prefer the four-volume *New International Dictionary of New Testament Theology* (*NIDNTT*), translated and
edited by Colin Brown from the German *Theologisches Be-
griffslexikon zum Neuen Testament*. Under Brown's editorship,
a team of conservative scholars expanded the original German work and provided a full bibliography in both English
and foreign languages. Arranged alphabetically in English,
the *NIDNTT* discusses some 340 key theological topics in the
New Testament. Its advantages over the *TDNT* are several:

   a. Its articles are more up to date.

b. Its word studies are midway between the concise definitions of a lexicon and the extensive discussions of the *TDNT*.
c. It represents the best in evangelical scholarship.
d. It frequently summarizes the discussions in the *TDNT*.
e. The text uses normal-sized print in contrast to the small print in the *TDNT*.
f. The total price of the *NIDNTT* is approximately one-third the price of the *TDNT*.

In addition, the third volume contains a valuable appendix by Murray J. Harris on the use of prepositions in the Greek New Testament. All these benefits make the *NIDNTT* one of the most usable tools for pastors and other students of Scripture.

6. A Concordance of Greek Words

Whereas lexicons describe vocabulary, concordances provide us with an alphabetical index of words, including references to the passages in the Bible in which each mention of a word occurs. New Testament concordances can be divided into two groups: those dealing with the Greek text directly and those dealing with an English translation.

It is an unfortunate but understandable fact that concordances based on the Greek New Testament are extremely expensive. For years the standard in the field has been *A Concordance to the Greek New Testament* by William F. Moulton and Alfred S. Geden, first published in 1897 and revised by Harold K. Moulton in 1978. Based on the text of Westcott and Hort (published in 1881), this volume contains longer Scripture quotations (in Greek) than do most concordances of its kind. It also contains references to the Septuagint and the Apocrypha, as well as citations in Hebrew if the passage in question is a quotation from the Old Testament. Most importantly, under a given word it often organizes the references by means of numbers that indicate special uses of the term. More recently, scholars have been turning to the *Computer-Konkordanz zum Novum Testamentum Graece*, edited by Horst Bachmann and Wolfgang A. Slaby. Based on the twenty-sixth edition of the Nestle–Aland Greek Testament, this beautifully produced concordance lists every New Testament word and its frequency of occurrence along with lengthy quotations of the passage in which the word is found. Both of these concordances may be profitably used in exegesis, though one may need access to a good theological library to do so.

All things considered, perhaps the most serviceable (and affordable) tool for pastors is Wigram's *Englishman's Greek Concordance of the New Testament*, which provides excellent coverage even though it is based on the superseded text behind the KJV. This concordance presents in alphabetical order every word that occurs in the Greek New Testament, along with the series of passages (quoted from the KJV) in which each word appears. The English word exhibiting the Greek word under consideration is always printed in italics. Adequate context in English is given, and the entries are fairly exhaustive. The main advantage of this concordance is that the student does not have to dig through the surrounding Greek text, which is likely to be unfamiliar. If one seeks more sophisticated word-study information, a theological dictionary of New Testament words (such as the *NIDNTT*) can be consulted.

The Englishman's Greek Concordance is undoubtedly one of the most useful tools you can have in your library. You can use it to compare the various ways a Greek word is translated in the New Testament, to examine the biblical development of an important doctrine, to locate significant parallel passages, or to do several other types of study. Though its text is outdated, having it is far better than having no concordance at all.

7. A New Testament Greek Grammar

Grammar involves study of the changes that individual words undergo as well as how words relate to each other when used together in sentences. One of the greatest hindrances to accurate exegesis is the over-simplified approach to grammar in first-year Greek courses. We are told that the aorist tense means "point action," that the first-class condition should be translated "since," that the present imperative always means to keep on doing something, and so forth. Each of these statements is potentially misleading, and none is completely accurate. This is why it is important to know more than the basics of the terminology and rules of Greek grammar.

The standard New Testament reference grammar is *A Greek Grammar of the New Testament and Other Early Christian Literature*, written by Friedrich Blass and Albert Debrunner and translated from the German by Robert W. Funk (hence the acronym BDF). The English translation includes a number of bibliographical additions and improves the organization of material within paragraphs. The preacher will find the index of passages cited useful in locating necessary information.

It is almost unnecessary to say that grammar touches exegesis at innumerable points. For example, some New Testament authors confuse εἰς and ἐν, while others keep them carefully apart. Hence preachers will be less apt to build a "theology of prepositions" once they see how much the New Testament writers differ in their usage of such words. The alert expositor will also wish to understand John's peculiar use of tense, especially his love for the perfect and pluperfect. Without a guide like BDF, we would lack this knowledge and be ignorant of a hundred other facts as well: for example, that αὐτός can mean simply "he," that ἴδιος is often no more than a substitute for τις, that some perfects (like ἤγγικα and πέποιθα) can have a present meaning, that ἵνα does not always mean "in order that," and so on. Knowledge of this kind brings deeper insight, sounder exegesis, and better preaching.

8. A Textual Commentary

There are over five thousand surviving manuscripts and fragments of the Greek New Testament, and many thousands more in other ancient languages. Not surprisingly, there are differences between the various Greek manuscripts. These differences are relatively insignificant in most places, and they affect only a small portion of the text of the New Testament. Nevertheless, in preparing sermons one will inevitably encounter alternate readings based on these differences. The Greek text behind the KJV, referred to as the *Textus Receptus* or the Received Text, is followed almost exclusively by that translation. On the other hand, most modern English versions are based on an eclectic (mixed) text determined by the translators themselves. These modern translations frequently differ from the KJV as much in their underlying Greek text as in their English style.

In chapter 4 we will deal in greater detail with the complicated science of textual criticism, which in recent years has enjoyed a revival of scholarly interest along with some spirited controversy. For those interested in more information about the subject, Bruce M. Metzger's *Text of the New Testament* is recommended as perhaps the standard textbook in the field today, though some will prefer J. Harold Greenlee's less technical *Introduction to New Testament Textual Criticism*. Pastors are not generally expected to become highly involved in this very technical field, but with a small amount of effort one can learn enough about textual criticism to follow the discussions in most commentaries.

Probably the most helpful tool for becoming familiar with the textual basis for the United Bible Societies' *Greek New Testament* is Metzger's *Textual Commentary on the Greek New Testament*. Those without formal training in textual criticism are strongly encouraged to read Metzger's introduction carefully and to glean as much as possible about the textual apparatus in the *GNT*. Metzger explains in nontechnical language the kinds of mistakes or changes copyists were most likely to have made to a text, shows how to evaluate a variant reading on the basis of external and internal criteria, and presents a partial listing of textually related witnesses to the text of the New Testament. This information is essential if one is to see how the editors of the *GNT* made a single Greek New Testament from several thousand manuscripts. The remainder of Metzger's book describes the major variants in the Greek text and offers summaries of the salient issues in each case. Speaking personally, I have rarely found a volume more useful than this one, even if I have frequently found myself disagreeing with its conclusions.

A word of caution is in order, however. At present, textual criticism is hardly an objective science. Some textual critics still follow Westcott and Hort in preferring the Alexandrian text type. This appears to be the case with the *GNT*, which some have labeled a new "Textus Receptus." Although the Alexandrian text type is indeed based on early and excellent manuscripts, it is often given an unjustifiably great weight in the selection of variants. This proclivity is also apparent in Metzger's *Textual Commentary*, where many of the decisions are said to be based on "better" external evidence, meaning the early Alexandrian text. Moreover, although the editors of the *GNT* would probably admit in theory that the Byzantine text can preserve an early reading, for all practical purposes readings of that text type are neglected as "debased" or "corrupt." Thus, instead of now relying too heavily on the Byzantine text (a characteristic of pre-nineteenth century scholarship), scholars today seem to rely too heavily on the Alexandrian text. Both extremes should be avoided.

9. A Synopsis of the Gospels

The fact that there are four accounts of the life of Christ requires us to think "horizontally," that is, to have an awareness of the parallels between the Gospels and an appreciation for the distinctives of any one Gospel. To obtain this awareness we must have access to a synopsis—a presentation of the Gospels in parallel columns. Though a synopsis must be regarded as merely approximate, it can give us an appreciation for the language and setting of any one Gospel in comparison with the others.

Most scholars keep at their elbows the *Synopsis Quattuor Evangeliorum*, edited by Kurt Aland. Its title simply means "Synopsis of the Four Gospels," indicating that it also includes the Gospel of John. This work contains a full textual apparatus based on the twenty-sixth edition of Nestle–Aland. One will also find here parallels from the early church fathers and a complete translation of the Gospel of Thomas.

Much more helpful for pastors, however, is the *Synopsis of the Four Gospels*, a Greek-English version of the above item. Also edited by Kurt Aland, this work lacks the parallels from the secondary literature but includes—to its great advantage—a literal English translation (the RSV) on facing pages. The synopsis itself reproduces each Gospel in its own sequence from beginning to end, each Gospel having its own column (in the canonical order Matthew, Mark, Luke, and John). A valuable apparatus at the bottom of the page shows variations in the major English translations. The book also contains a critical apparatus of Greek variants as listed in Nestle–Aland's twenty-sixth edition. In short, Aland's *Synopsis* is a technical triumph, offering a standard translation alongside the latest version of the Greek text.

That a "horizontal" reading of the Gospels is helpful can be seen from the following examination of the transfiguration account as recorded in Matthew 17:1–9, Mark 9:2–10, and Luke 9:28–36. By comparing these accounts, we discover that Luke's version is replete with memorable expressions that are unique to his story. Here is a sampling:

1. In keeping with the Lucan emphasis on prayer, Jesus goes up on the mountain "to pray" (9:28), and the transfiguration occurs while he "was praying" (9:29).

2. Luke clarifies the words "he was transfigured" (in Matthew and Mark) by explaining that "the appearance of his countenance was altered" (9:29).
3. Luke alone has Moses and Elijah speak with Jesus about his "departure" (ἔξοδος) at Jerusalem (9:31).
4. In Luke, Jesus is addressed as "Master" (9:33) instead of "Rabbi" (Mark) or "Lord" (Matthew).
5. The Greek word order of "listen to him" is emphatic only in Luke (αὐτοῦ ἀκούετε; 9:35).
6. Luke substitutes "Chosen One" (9:35) for Matthew's and Mark's "beloved" in the voice of the Father.

It is obvious that an understanding of Luke's account of the transfiguration requires an appreciation of these facts. The geographical identification of the Mount of Transfiguration—a question that preoccupies both archeologists and tourists to the Holy Land—does not interest Luke, since for him it is primarily a place of worship. Hence it is a *praying* Jesus who is transformed—a detail providing important implications for the transformation of the believer in Jesus (see Rom. 12:2). Moreover, Luke's more explicit description of Jesus' transfiguration ("the appearance of his countenance was altered") recalls Moses' experience in Exodus 34:29, where the latter's face was "glorified" on Mount Sinai during his encounter with the Lord. Luke's mention of Jesus' "departure" emphasizes both the Savior's death and his entire transit to the Father, the latter theme being a typical perspective of Lucan theology. The use of "Master" well suits the Lucan emphasis on the authority of Jesus, as do the words of the heavenly voice ("Chosen One" instead of "beloved"). All of this finds an appropriate climax in Luke's emphatic "to him listen!"—which contrasts the words of Jesus with those of the withdrawing figures of old (the implication being that the "Master" speaks with greater authority than both Moses and Elijah). Finally, in regard to the setting of Luke's account, the synopsis reveals that the transfiguration does not occur toward the end of Jesus' ca-

reer, nor is it located at Caesarea Philippi (features emphasized in Matthew and Mark). Instead, the transfiguration is
related to the Lucan geographical perspective: Jesus' movement toward Jerusalem, the city of destiny, echoes the exodus of Israel from Egypt to Canaan, the land of destiny.

The above insights into Luke's account of the transfiguration may also be gleaned from a modern critical commentary. A synopsis is still necessary, however, if only to check
on the accuracy of the commentators. You will discover
through experience that some distinctions among the Gospels are insignificant; but many of these differences highlight important theological emphases.

10. The Septuagint

All would-be interpreters of the New Testament will need
to have on hand a copy of the Septuagint, or the Greek Old
Testament (abbreviated LXX). The standard text is the *Septuaginta*, edited by Alfred Rahlfs and available from the
American Bible Society. Students desiring an English translation alongside the Greek may purchase *The Septuagint Version of the Old Testament and Apocrypha*. Pastors would do well
to become familiar with the Septuagint, since its influence
on the New Testament is seen in many areas. The Septuagint was the Bible for most of the New Testament writers,
and they took from it most of their citations of Scripture.
Matthew 13:14–15 and Romans 15:12 are examples of such
passages. Even the Book of Revelation, which does not contain direct quotations from the Old Testament, is permeated
with Old Testament language. Moreover, many New Testament theological terms, such as "law" (νόμος), "righteousness" (δικαιοσύνη), and "propitiation" (ἱλασμός), were taken
over directly from the Septuagint and must be understood
in the light of their use in that version. Hence the Septuagint is clearly relevant to New Testament exegesis, and both
the *TDNT* and the *NIDNTT* rightly acknowledge the Septuagint to be an important bridge between the Old Testament
and the New.

Expanding Your Library

Thus far we have covered basic reference works—those research tools that enable you to explore the depths of virtually any area of New Testament Greek studies. Although these resources are available in most college and seminary libraries, you would do well to have as many of them as possible in your personal library as well. This section continues with a consideration of books that are not necessarily essential but are nonetheless important.

In addition to BDF, several other New Testament Greek grammars deserve consideration. Students in my generation were weaned on Dana and Mantey's *Manual Grammar of the Greek New Testament*, which is still a popular intermediate grammar today and has the advantage of being eminently readable. I highly recommend it—provided it is supplemented by a book like C. F. D. Moule's *Idiom Book of New Testament Greek*, which surveys the major characteristics of New Testament Greek and discusses many difficult passages. Not to be overlooked, however, are the four volumes of *A Grammar of New Testament Greek*, by James H. Moulton, Wilbert F. Howard, and Nigel Turner. All four volumes are worth reading, but the third volume on syntax (by Turner) is definitely the most important. Finally, Maximilian Zerwick of the Pontifical Biblical Institute in Rome has produced a volume for seminarians entitled *Biblical Greek*. More a series of essays than a grammar, this book is often brilliant. Read Zerwick on the genitive and I think you will agree.

On lexicography, BAGD requires supplementation by a manual Greek lexicon. A "manual" lexicon is a "handy" tool, in contrast to a larger reference work. Without question, the best such lexicon is George Abbott-Smith's *Manual Greek Lexicon of the New Testament*, a compact dictionary offering basic definitions, etymologies, synonyms, and citations of Hebrew words underlying Greek usage. In addition, many students look to Abbott-Smith for its appendix of irregular Greek verbs.

Bible encyclopedias are books that attempt to shed light on various technical aspects of biblical studies. A good encyclopedia will include factual information, comprehensive summaries of specific subjects, and bibliographies for further study. The best of evangelical scholarship is represented in the *International Standard Bible Encyclopedia* (*ISBE*), now in its revised form. Written by recognized subject specialists and carefully edited by Geoffrey W. Bromiley, the new *ISBE* provides an excellent entry point for New Testament studies, and I refer to it frequently for its lucid presentations. Its four volumes are designed for the pastor, teacher, student, and even general reader—provided the reader is not daunted by technical discussions!

An introduction to the New Testament explains many problems of interpretation and discusses the books of the New Testament in turn. By any reckoning the best primer is Donald Guthrie's *New Testament Introduction*, though Everett F. Harrison's *Introduction to the New Testament*, Ralph P. Martin's *New Testament Foundations*, and Robert H. Gundry's *Survey of the New Testament* are not far behind. Whichever of these you choose, you will need to augment it with a work on New Testament backgrounds. Standard works in this field include F. F. Bruce's *New Testament History*, Bo Reicke's *New Testament Era*, and Merrill C. Tenney's *New Testament Times*. Bruce's volume is perhaps the most widely used of the three and far less expensive than anything else of its quality.

New Testament theology has much to contribute to Greek exegesis. Donald Guthrie's *New Testament Theology* wins kudos for comprehensiveness and readability (it includes frequent summaries), but there are also several briefer works that are useful, including George E. Ladd's *Theology of the New Testament* and Leon Morris's *New Testament Theology*. Students interested in a critique of recent developments in New Testament theology will find indispensable Gerhard F. Hasel's *New Testament Theology: Basic Issues in the Current Debate*.

Whose Greek vocabulary does not get rusty? Thankfully, publishers offer several resources designed to help students master their stock of New Testament words. The most useful of these are Bruce M. Metzger's *Lexical Aids for Students of New Testament Greek* and Robert E. Van Voorst's *Building Your New Testament Greek Vocabulary*. The former book lists the New Testament words by frequency of occurrence, while the latter volume offers a selection of Greek roots and the words derived from them. Van Voorst's work is excellent, but there is nothing like Metzger's *Lexical Aids* for completeness and usability.

Since New Testament exegesis involves a number of distinctive methods, students will need a guide through the current fashions in New Testament interpretation. A book written with attention to the needs of the beginning seminarian and the busy pastor is *New Testament Criticism and Interpretation*, edited by David Dockery and myself. It offers essays on New Testament interpretation by nineteen authors from sixteen evangelical seminaries and colleges. Each chapter is an exposition of a method or issue in New Testament interpretation along with examples from specific New Testament texts. The book represents the healthy shift away from confrontation between "faith" and "criticism," and could profitably be read in conjunction with its predecessor, *New Testament Interpretation*, edited by I. Howard Marshall.

Though frequently overlooked in seminary courses, special study aids are not to be disdained. An interlinear is a book that includes the Greek New Testament with a literal translation between the lines of the Greek text. There are numerous interlinears available today, including Marshall's and Berry's. In addition, a *Greek-English New Testament* is available from the American Bible Society, which has the Nestle–Aland Greek text and the RSV on facing pages. Another useful tool is Benjamin Chapman's *Greek New Testament Insert*, designed to be pasted in the back of the United Bible Societies' *Greek New Testament*. It includes the ABCs of

Greek grammar and an excellent section on syntax. Chapman has also produced laminated cards that fit in a three-ring binder showing basic elements of Greek morphology and syntax. Pierre Guillemette's *Greek New Testament Analyzed* contains the parsing of all the words in the *Greek New Testament*, including those in the critical apparatus.

Excellent information on exegesis and preaching can also be gleaned from periodicals or journals specializing in biblical studies. In my estimation, the exegetically minded pastor will profit most from the following: *Bibliotheca Sacra* (Dallas Seminary), *Criswell Theological Review* (Criswell College), *Interpretation* (Union Seminary), *Review and Expositor* (Southern Seminary), and the *Southwestern Journal of Theology* (Southwestern Seminary). Each of these journals keeps the interests of the preacher constantly in view, with an occasional glance in the direction of the scholar and the scholar-in-the-making.

Finally, several recent studies of New Testament Greek have attempted to take account of the methods and results of linguistics—the scientific study of language. Peter Cotterell and Max Turner's *Linguistics and Biblical Interpretation* will alert the reader to recent trends and will open the door to more ambitious works such as Moisés Silva's *Biblical Words and Their Meaning* and Johannes P. Louw's *Semantics of New Testament Greek*. My own *Linguistics for Students of New Testament Greek* is an attempt to set Greek grammar in the midst of the contemporary discussion (and debate). Of course, whether an integrative approach is the creature of the hour or a permanent development in Greek studies awaits a final answer.

When it comes to linguistic advances in the study of New Testament Greek, however, pride of place must go to Johannes P. Louw and Eugene A. Nida's two-volume *Greek-English Lexicon of the New Testament Based on Semantic Domains*. Not every lexicon generates as much enthusiasm for its subject as does this one. I doubt if there is a more compact essay on word meaning anywhere than in the lexicon's fourteen page introduction; and readers will profit immensely from the indexes in volume two. In between, the user will find the New Testament vocabulary arranged, not alphabetically, but under ninety-three "semantic domains," or fields of meaning among related words. The purpose of this new lexicon is to show how the New Testament words for a given concept compare and contrast with one another. The following words, for example, have related meanings and are found in the same part of the lexicon: νοῦς, καρδία, συνείδησις, φρήν, and πνεῦμα. Louw and Nida thus supplement BAGD by supplying important information not available elsewhere.

A Word on Computers

A good deal of research into the biblical texts with the aid of computers is now being carried on. Multilingual word processors that include Hebrew and Greek fonts now exist. In addition, the New Testament in Greek is available in several software packages. Certain routine aspects of sermon preparation can be carried out very effectively by using such software (e.g., word searches, displaying large blocks of text). The use of computers in grammatical analysis is yet another area of gain. For example, *Gramcord*, a grammatically based concordance of the Greek New Testament, facilitates both syntactical as well as morphological analysis. Word processing that involves foreign-language characters is now easily done. And the use of a shared network with other computers will assist speedy communication to and from most centers of learning. With its ability to store, retrieve, and edit at a moment's notice, the computer is a tool no preacher can afford to be without.

The pastor may find the following software packages particularly helpful in the preparation of sermons:

1. *CDWord*. A Bible research package containing four English translations of the Bible, the Greek Old and New

Testaments (including Apocrypha), two Bible dictionaries, three single-volume commentaries on the whole Bible, three Greek lexicons, and digitized graphics (i.e., maps and charts). A cross-referencing system links multiple resources together. Requires IBM computer and CD-ROM player. Available through Dallas Theological Seminary.

2. *Holy Bible.* Complete text of the Bible in three versions: NIV, RSV, and KJV (including Apocrypha for RSV and KJV). Requires any Mac and an 800 K drive. Available through Linguist's Software.

3. *MacBible.* A multilingual Bible program available in the NIV, KJV, NAB, and NRSV; includes the NIV Study Bible notes and the *Encyclopedia of Bible Difficulties.* Requires Mac Plus or larger, 1 MB of RAM, and an 800 K disk drive. Hard disk drive is recommended. Available through Zondervan Electronic Publishers.

4. *MacConcord I (KJV).* A concordance of the New Testament featuring a series of MacWrite documents containing more than ten thousand references from the KJV. Covers both theological and practical topics. Requires external disk drive or hard disk drive and MacWrite, Microsoft Word, or compatible word-processing program. Available through Medina Software.

5. *MacGreek New and Old Testaments.* Contains the United Bible Societies' *Greek New Testament* and the text of Rahlfs's edition of the Septuagint, including the full text of Codex Alexandrinus and Codex Vaticanus. Contains automatic nondeleting backspacing built into a single keystroke for breathing marks, accents, *iota* subscripts, dieresis, and combinations of these. Requires Microsoft Word and MacGreek or LaserGreek. Available through Linguist's Software.

6. *ScriptureFonts.* Includes Greek and Hebrew fonts for WordPerfect 5.0 and 5.1. Combines screen display, keyboard layouts, and printer fonts to support Hebrew

and Greek. Requires WordPerfect 5.0 or 5.1. Available through Zondervan Electronic Publishers.

7. *TLG Engine*. Requires access to the Thesaurus Linguae Graecae of the University of California at Irvine, a 58.5 million-word database of Greek literature before 600 A.D. The TLG Engine converts the database into Super-Greek ASCII code formatted for reading. Requires a Mac with 2 MB of RAM. Available through Linguist's Software.

8. *Verse Search V5*. Includes the entire text of the Bible with programs for searching for any English word or phrase. Available in the KJV, NIV, NKJV, RSV, NRSV, and *Reina Valera* (a Spanish version). The Greek transliteration allows access to the text of the KJV or NIV New Testament with Strong's reference numbers assigned to the English words. Requires Mac Plus or larger and 1 MB of RAM. Available through Bible Research Systems.

Conclusion

All of us who preach regularly know we should study more often than we do. We also know there are unlimited obstacles in our way. The major impediment is the amount of time and energy involved. It seems that the hardest burden in a preacher's life is finding time for personal study. The sins and temptations of the pastor's study are legion. As an incumbent sinner, I have more often than I like to admit been brought up short by my own lack of fortitude and constancy. The whole purpose of the room we call the "study," however, is to study. Let the pastor start listening to the radio or glancing at the paper, and serious exegesis is as good as dead.

Other preachers with whom I have shared this somewhat grim assessment assure me that I have not overstated their plight. Most pastors today have three jobs: pastoral care, administration, and preaching. Each one requires a different set of skills, and each one, done properly, could be a full-time job. It is obvious that pastors cannot spend all their time studying and still be administrators, counselors, organizers, and so on. Yet no pastor can ignore serious study. The Christian faith was given to be examined, pondered, taught, preached, and energetically preserved. And it is abundantly clear that exegesis is a vital element in all this activity. Hence no pastor can justify demoting the earnest study of God's Word from the place of top priority among the tasks of the pastoral calling.

To sum up, the more I preach, the more I am convinced that private study must be balanced by the collected wisdom of the ages. We may be tempted to think that understanding Scripture requires nothing more than the illuminating work of the Holy Spirit ("Since I have the Holy Spirit, why do I need to know the twelve uses of the genitive case?"). The Holy Spirit, however, does not impart information that we can acquire for ourselves. Haddon W. Robinson has well said, "Accuracy, not to speak of integrity, demands that we develop every possible skill to keep us from declaring in the name of God what the Holy Spirit never intended to convey."[3] Is that not reason enough to get these books off the shelf and into ourselves?

Stop and Think

Which of the reference tools mentioned in this chapter do you currently own? Are there any tools you would add to our list? Prepare a list of "priority" tools you would like to purchase for yourself.

---

3. Haddon W. Robinson, *Biblical Preaching: The Development and Delivery of Expository Messages* (Grand Rapids: Baker, 1980), p. 59.

3

Getting Oriented

The Nature and Task of Greek Exegesis

Exegesis is an essential task of the church. It exists to point men and women to Christ and the kingdom. This fact, more than any other, has retained for the Bible a central place in the curriculum of evangelical seminaries. Apart from the Word of God read and studied, examined and expressed with clarity in preaching and teaching, the church ceases to be the church, formed and reformed by that Word. Instead it begins to talk to itself, echoing the language of the world and degenerating into self-centered piety.

Unfortunately—and often owing to confusion in the seminaries themselves—ministers frequently are uncertain about their task as exegetes of Holy Scripture. The recent proliferation of books on biblical hermeneutics has demonstrated how difficult it is to arrive at an adequate definition of what it means to "interpret the Bible." Much work remains to be done, and even in the evangelical camp there are several paths one might usefully follow. Yet for all the valid insights of recent books on evangelical hermeneutics, it is an inescapable fact that professional opinion is still very

much divided on the nature and task of exegesis. It is plain
that the emphasis on the various facets of interpretation
(historical, grammatical, syntactical, structural, theological,
etc.) will shift from one age to another and from one dominant culture to another.

All this is simply to state that scholars are never wholly
dispassionate about their methodology. They inevitably
bring to their work a mass of presuppositions that belong to
the tradition in which they were raised and educated.
Above all, they cannot long pretend to have found a final,
irreducible, and unchanging definition of their task. All that
anyone who writes on the topic of exegesis can hope to ac-
complish is to take the tradition that he or she has received
and apprehended and attempt to relate it to the wider community of faith. Hence at several critical junctures I have
come to rather personal conclusions, and the reader is
urged to deal as critically as possible with the material presented here. Nevertheless, it may still be possible to reach
agreement on at least the broad parameters of what is involved in doing exegesis for today's church. With that goal
in mind, the following section will attempt to provide a
working definition of exegesis as a basis for a fuller discussion later.

Toward a Definition of Exegesis

Let me begin by posing three questions we will want to
ask ourselves every time we sit down to study a New Testament passage:

1. Do I know where my text fits biblically?
2. Am I really certain about what the text is saying?
3. Could anyone benefit from what I have to say about
   the text?

These three questions, it seems to me, are the exegetically
crucial ones. The issues are always the same: Do I have an

informed understanding of the text, both in light of its original setting and in view of its modern applicability? Anyone engaged in expository preaching inevitably raises these basic questions. There is, moreover, a logical order in the way we raise them. We do not begin by asking, "What *does* this text mean?" but instead, "What *did* it mean?" Somehow we sense that a text, be it the Bible or a modern novel, must be understood in light of its own historical setting. On the other hand, we also sense that it is improper to stop with questions of what the text meant, for Scripture in the end drives us to ask the question of how its light can be brought to bear on contemporary problems.

In a visually oriented age like ours, it may be helpful to look at these questions in geometric terms. Exegesis involves approaching the text from three different yet interrelated angles. First, in exegesis we look *at* the text, interrogating it rigorously to discern its biblical and historical setting. "Looking at" implies that we stand "above" the text, attempting to gain a bird's-eye view of the whole. Second, as exegetes we must also look *inside* the text, standing "within" it and drawing out its meaning by using all available philological tools. Exegesis is designed to further this step by establishing proper rules and procedures for grammatical interpretation. Third, exegesis is not complete until we look *beyond* the text, for our task as preachers is not to understand Scripture for its own sake, but to interpret it for modern listeners, ourselves included. At this point we stand "under" the text, ready to obey it and to proclaim it in a way that makes personal and significant its saving truth.

The interpreter committed to biblical preaching will always be found standing "above," "within," and "under" the text. These three perspectives comprise the essence of the exegetical task. Put less graphically, there are three basic areas of discovery in exegesis, which we might now call context, meaning, and significance. The questions of *context* are both historical and literary. Historical context has to do with the religious, political, and cultural situation facing the author and the original audience. Literary context deals with the way in which the text fits into its immediate surroundings as well as with the formal character (genre) of the document in which the text is found. The questions of *meaning* are basically of six kinds: textual (dealing with the original wording), lexical (dealing with the meaning of words), syntactical (dealing with the relationship of words to one another), structural (dealing with the overall arrangement of the text), rhetorical (dealing with the relationship of form to meaning), and tradition-critical (dealing with the traditions behind and within the text). Finally, the questions of *significance* involve two matters: theology (what we hear) and proclamation (what we preach).

I have said enough about the exegetical process to move to an outline for exegesis using the concepts discussed above. Other approaches are of course possible—one of the intriguing aspects of exegesis is knowing where to place the emphasis—but this is one way we may view our task:

1. The view from "above"   **Where do we find our text?**

   a. Historical analysis   What was the situation facing the author and readers?

   b. Literary analysis   How does the text contribute to the whole book?

2. The view from "within"   **What did our text convey to its first readers?**

   a. Textual analysis   What is the original text?

   b. Lexical analysis   What are the significant words in the text?

   c. Syntactical analysis   How are the words related to one another?

   d. Structural analysis   How did the author arrange the text?

   e. Rhetorical analysis   How did the author use form to communicate meaning?

f. Tradition analysis	How did the author utilize previous traditions in the text?
3. The view from "under"	**How does our text apply to modern life?**
a. Theological analysis	What biblical truth is apparent in the text?
b. Homiletical analysis	How do I best proclaim this truth?

It will be clear by now that the exegete's work involves a series of distinct yet interdependent disciplines. Though the text is fixed as to its place in the biblical canon, quite frequently there are historical and literary uncertainties of some significance for interpretation. Hence the exegete must give some thought to establishing the historical setting of the text as well as the general character of the writing in which the text appears. Next, the exegete's linguistic competence comes into play in an effort to understand the text itself. Finally, the interpreter aims at appreciating the message of the author and its relevance for the modern reader.

To summarize, then, exegesis begins with an accurate knowledge of the biblical setting of the text. No text can be interpreted apart from a consideration of these historical and literary factors that are, in a sense, extraneous to the text itself, but are nonetheless essential for understanding its meaning. In the next place, exegesis requires an accurate understanding of the text itself, to be acquired by careful study of the author's thought as expressed through written words. Finally, exegesis requires an ample knowledge of life experience so that the exegesis may be directed toward meaningful application and not just toward the impartation of facts about the text.

Preaching, too, shares these three dimensions. In has a *historical* dimension, for it puts people in touch with an ancient tradition reaching back all the way to the early church and even beyond that to the life of Jesus himself. It has a *grammatical* dimension, because it assists people in entering and making sense of the author's thought-world in its own right. And it has a *personal* dimension, because the goal is the individual appropriation of the message that is preached and heard. Thus, by standing "above" the text as a distanced observer, "within" the text as a diligent interpreter, and "under" the text as a devoted disciple, the preacher is enabled to interpret the text responsibly for the modern listener.

The Value of Exegesis

Granted that the above analysis is a fairly accurate description of the exegetical task, does that solve the problem of hermeneutics? Hardly. In the course of teaching exegesis I have more than once heard the comment: "This sounds interesting, but is all of this really necessary to understand a text?" This question does not spring from any polemical intentions; on the contrary, ministerial students are justifiably wary of any form of "criticism" that might undermine the authority of Scripture. I share that concern. As important as exegesis is, it can actually hamper preaching if the approach becomes a kind of grammaticalism that is irrelevant or peripheral to understanding and communicating the meaning of the text.

I am convinced, however, that if we do our exegetical work responsibly we need not be concerned about undermining our faith—or anyone else's. Instead of fearing exegesis, we should recognize that much of our work in the text is homiletical in orientation and that the various components of exegesis have relevance for and can be carried over to the modern-day application of the text. Before progressing any further, then, it might be helpful to identify some of the practical aspects of the exegetical methods discussed above.

Discovering the Text

Historical Analysis

Basic to all competent exegesis is the study of historical and literary context. Typical concerns of historical analysis include author, audience, date, occasion, purpose, cultural and sociological influences, and all other related background matters. Sensitivity to these matters does not call for yawn-producing lectures on ancient history; a brief explanation of the most important details will suffice. For example, Francis Schaeffer introduces his sermon on "The Water of Life" (John 7:1–39) with the following historical remarks:

> The Feast of the Tabernacles was so named because God had commanded the Jews to live in tabernacles during this period each year to remind them that they had had to live in temporary abodes as they moved through the wilderness after the exodus. Through the centuries since then and still today, the Jews have enacted this reminder. During the wanderings, God twice provided water from a rock, so the feast reenacted this, too. In fact the remembrance of this had developed as a technical part of the festival and had tremendous importance. On the final day, "the great day of the feast," came the great rite of pouring out water in the presence of the people to represent God's provision in the desert. Non-biblical sources reveal that the force of the fervor that built up as people waited for this outpouring, the sheer religiosity of the situation, was almost unbearable. As the water poured out, the Feast came to its close.[1]

It was precisely at this point, continues Schaeffer, that Jesus stood up and announced to all in attendance, "If anyone is thirsty, let him come to me and drink. The one who believes in me, as the Scripture has said, out of his innermost being will flow rivers of living water" (John 7:37–38 NASB modi-

1. Francis A. Schaeffer, *No Little People: Sixteen Sermons for the Twentieth Century* (Downers Grove, Ill.: InterVarsity, 1974), p. 213.

fied). Here the entire sermon is dictated by the historical elements surrounding the Feast of Tabernacles. Although not every message can or should be so tied to history, in this instance to fail to locate Jesus' ministry in the period of this feast would be fatal to an appropriate understanding of his words.

Not only the Gospel of John, but each New Testament writing requires a knowledge of the historical situation from which it stems. For instance, most of the New Testament letters deal with specific situations or problems that arose in the churches being addressed. The purpose of courses in New Testament Introduction is to provide the necessary background information about these writings: Who wrote the text? When and where was it written? To whom was it written? Although this type of information may appear dull or irrelevant, it is indispensable if the text is to be heard in terms of its original setting. Hence "New Testament Introduction" has far-reaching implications for the study of specific New Testament texts.

Literary Analysis

In addition to the matter of historical context discussed above, literary context also demands attention. Usually three levels of literary analysis are recognized: the canonical, the remote, and the immediate. The canonical context is the text's place in the Bible itself. The remote context embraces paragraphs, a chapter, or even an entire book of Scripture. The immediate context consists of those verses or paragraphs that immediately precede or follow the text.

That careful attention to literary context benefits preaching should stand beyond need for demonstration. In his book *Biblical Preaching*, Haddon W. Robinson reminds us that "setting the passage within its wider framework simply gives the Bible the same chance we give the author of a paperback."[2] Yet the same person who would never read just

2. Haddon W. Robinson, *Biblical Preaching: The Development and Delivery of Expository Messages* (Grand Rapids: Baker, 1980), p. 58.

a single paragraph from an Ernest Hemingway novel would think nothing of fragmentizing the Bible along the lines of his or her own subjective predilections. Countless people have memorized individual verses of Scripture without realizing that verses are only components of a larger context. For example, Romans 3:23 is only part of a sentence, yet we know only that part and forget the rest. Similarly, the promise of divine assistance in Hebrews 13:5b ("I will never leave you or forsake you") is meaningless if we ignore the commands of verse 5a: "Keep your lives free from the love of money, and be content with what you have" (NRSV). More to the point, there exists a dangerous trend in contemporary preaching to drag the text, kicking and screaming, out of its surroundings and into the pulpit. We can partly blame this fragmentizing tendency on the French printer Robert Estienne (Stephanus), whose versified edition of the Greek New Testament (1551) left the erroneous impression that every verse stands on its own, apart from the surrounding context. The King James Version (1611) followed suit, and modern versions unwittingly perpetuate this distortion.

In his exposition of James 3, J. W. MacGorman adeptly demonstrates both the importance and homiletical use of each contextual level mentioned above.[3] His theme is the control of the tongue. MacGorman begins by noting how this theme was common in Jewish wisdom literature, especially the Book of Proverbs. Standing in this tradition, James too was concerned about the sins of the tongue. MacGorman then moves to the remote context, showing how James's exhortation on the tongue is rooted in his earlier admonitions: believers should be slow to speak (1:19); human wrath does not work divine righteousness (1:20); religion that does not enable believers to control their speech is vain (1:26); Christians are to speak with an aware-

3. See J. W. MacGorman, "An Exposition of James 3," *Southwestern Journal of Theology* 29 (1986), pp. 31–36.

ness that they will soon be judged by God for what they
have said (2:12). MacGorman concludes by showing how
James's warning was specifically directed to certain persons
who were rashly presuming upon the teaching office of the
church (3:1–12). MacGorman's entire exposition is virtually an object lesson on the levels of context in preaching. The
full meaning of the text becomes available only as the parts
of the text interact with one another.

At least two implications for preaching follow from this
overview of contextual analysis. The first is that the selected preaching text should be a single unit. In general, therefore, preaching texts should be chosen only after the entire
book has been studied and outlined. The second implication is that the preaching text should not be a combination
of passages from various books. This does not mean, of
course, that one may not consider parallel texts. But to
preach from several texts at once can hardly do justice to
the unique historical and literary context of each passage of
Scripture. It is very clear that proof-texting has no place in
exegesis. As Walter C. Kaiser states, "'proof texting,' the
isolation and use of verses apart from their immediate or
sectional context, is reprehensible and should be discontin-
ued immediately."[4]

Understanding the Text

If sound interpretation demands a study of historical and
literary context, it also requires a careful grammatical analysis of the passage under consideration. New Testament
scholars have done much to advance our knowledge of this
aspect of exegesis, and the subject can become highly technical and complex. But the analysis is necessary. Only
through careful study of the passage itself can we understand the original meaning of the text without reading into
it our own ideas drawn from the present.

4. Walter C. Kaiser Jr., *Toward an Exegetical Theology: Biblical Exegesis for Preaching and Teaching* (Grand Rapids: Baker, 1981), p. 82.

Textual Analysis

There is no necessary order in the exegetical process, but determining the best available text is a logical place to start. When the interpreter discovers alternative wording within the Bible, textual analysis comes into play. Textual analysis may be defined as an attempt to determine the original wording of a document. New Testament textual analysis is necessary because the existing Greek manuscripts vary among themselves to a considerable degree. These differences in the Greek manuscripts are reflected frequently enough in the major English versions that the expositor will inevitably be called upon to make an informed judgment. For example, some editions of the NASB put Luke 23:17 in brackets, with a footnote stating, "Many mss. do not contain this v." The homiletical task cannot avoid the question of whether or not this verse should be preached.

Textual analysis is also essential for determining the wording within individual verses. In Matthew 5:22, for example, the words *without a cause* are absent in the majority of modern English versions, though this reading is found in the KJV. Did Jesus forbid *all* anger or only *unjustified* anger? Most scholars feel that the word εἰκῇ (without a cause) was added to soften Jesus' strong teaching, but an equally strong case can be made for the inclusion of the word on the basis that it was liable to be understood as being too indulgent to anger. Obviously an informed understanding of this textual problem is necessary before one preaches from this portion of the Sermon on the Mount.[5]

Lexical Analysis

After determining the original text, the exegete must attempt to determine the meaning of the words within the text. This is the fundamental concern of lexical analysis (word study). Often considered the "Open Sesame" to the

---

5. I have discussed the complexities of this variant in my essay "Jesus on Anger: The Text of Matthew 5:22a Revisited," *Novum Testamentum* 30 (1988), pp. 1–8.

original meaning of Scripture, lexical analysis is perhaps more open to abuse than any other method of interpretation. New Testament scholars have become painfully aware in recent years that even the extensive analyses contained in the ten-volume *Theological Dictionary of the New Testament* do not always give full and sufficient recognition to the influence of the particular context on the meaning of a word. Nevertheless, word study is of great benefit to exegesis, especially when the interpreter is careful to see how the word has actually been put to work in the service of concrete expression.

The preacher will occasionally find sermonic illustrations growing from lexical seeds imbedded in the text. Consider Galatians 1:8–9, where Paul uses the word ἀνάθεμα (accursed) for the fate of the false teachers. In ancient literature the word was sometimes used of votive offerings set up in temples and at other times of something delivered up for destruction. This same double sense lay behind the Hebrew word *ḥērem* (חֵרֶם), which is frequently translated in the Septuagint by ἀνάθεμα. In Deuteronomy 7:25–26 ἀνάθεμα (and *ḥērem*) is applied to the graven images of the Canaanite gods, and in Joshua 6:17–19 it is applied to Jericho. In the New Testament ἀνάθεμα occurs six times to denote the object of a curse and only once in the sense of a votive offering (in a variant reading found in Luke 21:5). Here in Galatians it seems to refer to the delivering up to the wrath of God of those who are "accursed" because they proclaim a false gospel. At this point the preacher is practically assaulted with applications. People may masquerade as evangelists in an outward conformity to religious regulations, but may actually be objects of God's wrath as perverters of the gospel of Christ!

Sometimes an introductory sermon on an entire book of the New Testament may be prodded by a single Greek word. The final word in the Greek text of Acts is ἀκωλύτως (unhindered). This word also appears at crucial points in the narrative and epitomizes a major theme in Acts: that the good news of salvation in Jesus is "unhindered" by such barriers as ethnic identity, language, geography, and religious rites. Contrary to popular opinion, Acts does not merely tell us how the gospel got from Jerusalem to Rome. Just as importantly, it tells us how Paul, languishing in prison for preaching in a way offensive to the exclusivism of Judaism, could still openly proclaim that message.

Although lexical analysis is important, it is a limited tool, a servant rather than the sovereign. As a professor of Greek, I have never worried much about my students' ability to do word studies; I am always far more anxious that they will stop there. Too much New Testament preaching tends to be "word bound" and to ignore the broader context in which words are found. James Barr in particular has stressed the significance of context in exegesis: "It is the sentence (and of course the still larger literary complex such as the complete speech or poem) which is the linguistic bearer of the usual theological statement, and not the word (the lexical unit)."[6] What Barr is saying is that the uniqueness of the New Testament is not found in the issuing of new "Christian" words, but in new combinations of words. This point is neatly summed up in the story of the sheik who wished to give an employee a present. The intended beneficiary suggested, "Perhaps a few golf clubs." Later the recipient received a telegram that said, "Have bought you Pebble Beach and am negotiating for the Rivicra." The employee, of course, had meant the implements used in playing the game!

Syntactical Analysis

When lexical analysis has exhausted its usefulness, it is time to go on to syntactical analysis. Syntax involves sensitivity to clauses and other sense units that are larger than individual words. It also includes such matters of the tense, voice, mood, person, number, and case of individual words.

6. James Barr, *The Semantics of Biblical Language* (Oxford: Oxford University Press, 1961), p. 263.

Since syntax is essential to the study of an author's thought patterns, it is here that Greek has a particularly useful role to play. Flow of thought cannot be determined by the English structure, not even in a literal translation. Moreover, syntactical problems frequently arise even in the original Greek, and such problems are rarely apparent in translation. For these reasons, although a knowledge of Greek is important in lexical analysis, it is essential in syntactical analysis.

Here, again, the Greek text offers numerous examples of exegesis in action. Frequently the tense of a Greek verb will affect meaning in an important way. For example, when the preacher working from 1 Corinthians 15:3–4 reads that Christ died (ἀπέθανεν), was buried (ἐτάφη), was seen (ὤφθη), but *has been* raised (ἐγήγερται), that preacher uncovers a dimension of the gospel basic to all New Testament preaching but buried in most translations. "Has been raised" renders a Greek perfect tense verb, accentuating the permanence of the resurrection and its consequences in contrast to the impermanence of Christ's death, burial, and appearances.

Sometimes an entire sermon can be rooted in Greek syntax. In his message on Ephesians 5:18 entitled "The Command to be Filled with the Spirit," W. A. Criswell begins with a word study of "fill" (πληρόω) and compares it with several of its New Testament synonyms.[7] The body of the sermon then evolves directly from the grammatical nuances of the verb πληροῦσθε (be filled):

1. God commands that we be filled with the Spirit (the verb is in the imperative mood).
2. This filling is a repeated experience (the verb is in the present tense).
3. We must yield ourselves to the influence of the Spirit (the verb is in the passive voice).

7. W. A. Criswell, *The Holy Spirit in Today's World* (Grand Rapids: Zondervan, 1966), pp. 132–36.

In this sermon Greek syntax has laid a firm foundation, like steel rods embedded within concrete. Whether or not every sermon is so pervasively grammatical, the preacher is no less obligated to practice responsible syntactical analysis.

Knowledge of Greek syntax can also be an important factor in the exegesis of problem passages. Hebrews 6:4–6, for example, describes the defection of professing Christians. Is repentance impossible for these people, even if they show a willingness to repent? Here Greek syntax offers hope, for the force of the present tense participles in verse 6 suggests that such apostates can be reclaimed unless they persist in "crucifying" (ἀνασταυροῦντας) and "ridiculing" (παραδειγματίζοντας) the Son of God. In other words, the author seems to be saying that the one who *consistently* disowns Christ is ultimately disowned by him.

Structural Analysis

Once the interpreter has reached a decision about the wording and syntax of the passage under consideration, other questions arise that have to do with the text's larger composition. If syntax is concerned with the meaning of words in their combination with other words, structural analysis is concerned with the ways clauses and larger thought units are placed in relation with each other. Since it is difficult to say what *anything* means until one has decided in a sense what *everything* means, the study of structure is an indispensable component of exegesis. This structure cannot be translated into another language, because translators must use the grammatical system of the target language. If interpreters use only an English translation, they are often reduced to guessing at the important distinction between main points and secondary points in the original text.

Quite often the interpreter will find diagramming a passage helpful for determining its structure. This procedure involves rewriting the passage in order to see how the parts fit the whole. Haddon W. Robinson calls the tool for deter-

mining the structure of a passage a "mechanical layout,"
while Walter C. Kaiser favors the term "syntactical display."
Gordon D. Fee prefers the title "sentence flow schematic,"
and provides several suggestive examples for study. Perhaps
the most helpful approach is Johannes P. Louw's method of
"colon analysis," which itself is based on the practice of the
ancient Greeks.[8] What is important, however, is not the
name but the need for the student to view the passage in
terms of its basic sense units and its overall composition.

How can structural analysis bring clarity to preaching?
One way is in terms of homiletical construction. The best
sermon outlines flow directly from the structure of the text
itself. The following analysis of Hebrews 12:1–2 demonstrates how the preacher can get in touch with the text
through an awareness of its structure.[9]

τοιγαροῦν καὶ ἡμεῖς δι᾽ ὑπομονῆς **τρέχωμεν** τὸν προκείμενον ἡμῖν
ἀγῶνα
   τοσοῦτον **ἔχοντες** περικείμενον ἡμῖν νέφος μαρτύρων
   ὄγκον **ἀποθέμενοι** πάντα καὶ τὴν εὐπερίστατον ἁμαρτίαν
   ἀφορῶντες εἰς τὸν τῆς πίστεως ἀρχηγὸν καὶ τελειωτὴν Ἰησοῦν
     ὃς ἀντὶ τῆς προκειμένης αὐτῷ χαρᾶς ὑπέμεινεν σταυρὸν
     αἰσχύνης καταφρονήσας ἐν δεξιᾷ τε τοῦ θρόνου τοῦ θεοῦ
     κεκάθικεν

therefore **let us run** with endurance the race set before us
   having so great a cloud of witnesses surrounding us
   laying aside every encumbrance and the easily entan-
   gling sin
   fixing our eyes on Jesus the author and perfecter of
   faith

8. Robinson, *Biblical Preaching*, p. 68; Kaiser, *Toward an Exegetical Theology*,
p. 99; Gordon D. Fee, *New Testament Exegesis: A Handbook for Students and Pastors*
(Philadelphia: Westminster, 1983), p. 61; Johannes P. Louw, *Semantics of New Testament Greek* (Philadelphia: Fortress/Chico, Calif.: Scholars Press, 1982), p. 95.

9. See further my essay "A Note on the Structure of Hebrews 12:1–2," *Biblica*
68 (1987), pp. 543–51.

who for the joy set before him endured the cross
and despising the shame sat down at the right hand of
the throne of God

Here the basic thought units jump out like the white lines
on an athletic field. The theme is brought out to the left,
while the more subordinate elements cluster to the right.
From the first line of the analysis, which alone contains an
independent finite verb (τρέχωμεν), we can immediately see
the author's main point: running the race with endurance.
Thereafter come three participial clauses that qualify the
"race": (1) it is by the knowledge that others have finished
the race that the present generation of runners can expect
to complete it; (2) no runner, however, can hope to attain
the goal without an abhorrence of personal sin; and (3) the
runner must look to Jesus, "the author and perfecter of
faith." The remaining items are a description of Jesus,
showing how the main theme of "running the race" climax-
es in "Jesus and who he is." By reducing these elements to
an outline, the preacher can move directly from structural
analysis to sermon construction:

Text: Hebrews 12:1–2

Title: Run to Win!

Theme: The Christian is called on to follow the example of
               Christ into a life of submission and obedience ("let us
               run with endurance")

Outline: I. Our Encouragement ("having so great a cloud of
                 witnesses")

                 II. Our Entanglements ("laying aside every encum-
                 brance")

                 III. Our Example ("fixing our eyes on Jesus")

This simple outline clearly demonstrates how by analyzing
the Greek text the preacher can move from theory to practice. In shaping one's outline by the contours of the text's

internal structure, one can emphasize the dominant thoughts of the author without majoring on the minors or reading into the text one's favorite subject. This is not to say that every sermon will take its form directly from the form of the text. But a sermon should never violate the spirit of the form of the text. Jesus' parables, for instance, were never designed for the straitjacket of deductive reasoning imposed on them by succeeding generations of preachers. Yet the form of the text will often suggest a clue to the form of the sermon, even if the final shape of the sermon is determined by other considerations.

Rhetorical Analysis

When we turn from structural analysis and begin to look at the literary dimensions of a passage, we encounter the field of rhetorical analysis. Although originally applied mainly to the Old Testament, rhetorical analysis is a welcome and much needed supplement to New Testament study. Rhetorical analysis is essentially an attempt to clarify our understanding of the biblical text through a study of its literary techniques. Ancient authors often employed these techniques in order to assist readers to understand the message of the text or to persuade them of the truth of the presentation. As the art of reading a text, rhetorical analysis involves close attention to the scope of a given passage (its beginning and end), the discovery of figures of speech (e.g., simile and metaphor), the observation of compositional techniques (e.g., parallelism and chiasmus), and judgments about the relationship of form to meaning. Hence the interpreter should always allow for the possibility that the rhetorical dimension of the text will bear directly on exegetical questions.

In the last two decades the rhetorical features of the New Testament have been explored with increasing frequency. In 1 John 2:12–14, for example, the three groups represented by τεκνία/παιδία (children), πατέρες (fathers), and νεανίσκοι (young men) have troubled commentators from the earliest centuries. But when identified with the rhetorical figure of *distributio*, the passage becomes more intelligible.[10] In *distributio*, the inclusive group is listed first and is then "distributed" into constituent groups. Thus "children" is the inclusive term, which is then followed by an address to the spiritually mature in the congregation ("fathers") and the spiritual novices ("young men"). This conclusion is further supported by Johannine usage, since in John the terms τεκνία and παιδία are reserved for all the faithful, whereas neither πατέρες nor νεανίσκοι is ever used of an entire audience. Here the rhetorically minded preacher might allow the sermon to share the text's characteristic of first describing the entire church before addressing the two groups of believers that are inevitably present in any congregation.

Rhetorical criticism is a well-watered garden in which a variety of promising seeds have been planted and where a considerable growth can even now be seen. But to reap any fruit the interpreter must be willing to tarry lovingly in the text; beauty usually eludes the casual observer. For example, we noted earlier how the structure of Hebrews 12:1–2 calls attention to the person and work of Christ. Now observe how this focus is confirmed by the rhetorical structure of the text:

A   having *seated* around us such a great cloud of witnesses
B   *setting aside* every weight and clinging sin
C   with *patient endurance*
D   let us run the race *that is set before us*
X   **fixing our eyes on Jesus the author and perfecter of faith**
D′   who for the joy *that was set before him*
C′   *patiently endured* the cross
B′   *scorning* the shame
A′ and has *taken his seat* at the right hand of the throne of God

10. See Duane F. Watson, "1 John 2:12–14 as *Distributio, Conduplutio*, and *Expolitio*: A Rhetorical Understanding," *Journal for the Study of the New Testament* 35 (1989), pp. 97–110.

In rhetoric this device is known as a chiasmus—an inverted parallelism in which the center line receives the emphasis. Discovery of this pattern is not only an indication of the author's literary artistry, but shows the interrelationship between the individual lines of the passage and calls attention to the centerpiece of the entire paragraph ("fixing our eyes on Jesus"). A similar analysis might well be printed in the church bulletin when one is preaching from this passage in order to enable the congregation to be led along in a deeper understanding of the text.

Tradition Analysis

The five methods of analysis discussed above are the most important approaches for understanding a biblical text. However, several other methods provide additional insights and should also be mentioned here. These methods are commonly treated as types of "criticism," which is a fitting word provided it is not saddled with antibiblical nuances. Originally regarded with some suspicion in evangelical circles, these methods have become increasingly acceptable as exegetical tools.[11]

For the sake of convenience, we will subsume these critical approaches under the label of tradition analysis. Tradition analysis, as used here, is concerned with such matters as the identity and extent of sources that may lie behind a given work, the possible composite nature of a book, and the contributions of an author to the traditions that were utilized in composing a given work. Tradition analysis has shown how the books of the New Testament are sometimes the final products of long and complex processes of compiling, writing, and editing. Biblical scholars generally study these aspects of tradition analysis under the headings of source, form, and redaction criticism.

11. On the place of higher criticism in New Testament studies, see David Alan Black and David S. Dockery (eds.), *New Testament Criticism and Interpretation* (Grand Rapids: Zondervan, 1991).

The first method, *source criticism,* was developed between
1863 and 1924. It seeks to answer the question, "How much
of the New Testament material was already in existence before the writers set about their task?" Preexisting tradition
may range from the simple confession "Jesus is Lord"
(1 Cor. 12:3) to the detailed summary of the gospel in
1 Corinthians 15:3–5. Most evangelical source critics work
on the assumption that a high proportion of the material in
the Synoptic Gospels (Matthew, Mark, and Luke) came
from literary sources. Source critics also study the possible
literary interdependence between these Gospels. The dominant hypothesis explaining the literary relationships between Matthew, Mark, and Luke is called the "Two-
Document Hypothesis" because it posits the priority of
Mark, with its subsequent use by Matthew and Luke, plus
the existence of a sayings source (called "Q") also used by
Matthew and Luke. Alternative theories—which argue either for the priority of Matthew or of Luke—make synoptic
criticism exceedingly complex but not, thereby, irrelevant
for exegesis. At its simplest, source criticism demands that
we take seriously the high degree of originality shown by all
these evangelists, an originality so great that any one of the
Synoptic Gospels can be viewed as having been written first!

A movement arising directly out of source criticism and
based on it is *form criticism,* which was developed between
the two world wars. The purpose of form criticism is to go
behind the sources used by the evangelists to the period of
oral transmission (A.D. 30–50) and to isolate and analyze
the individual literary units in the synoptic tradition. These
units, called "pericopes," can be classified into categories
such as parables, miracle stories, stories about Jesus, woes,
and the like. In addition to genre classification, form criticism is also concerned with assessing the function of a per-
icope in the life of the early church. A basic assumption of
form criticism is that the very preservation of the tradition
about Jesus influenced the form in which it was cast. When
a question arose about Sabbath observance, or about

divorce, or about any number of issues, it was natural to remember what Jesus had said or taught on the subject. Iso-
lating these units of the primitive tradition and discovering
their usage in the life of the church helps the interpreter
gain an appreciation of the sociological and liturgical dimensions underneath the text. Thus, for example, it is possible that the story of the Syrophoenecian woman (Mark
7:24–30) may have been remembered originally in answer
to the question, "How did Jesus treat those outside of Judaism?" It is this "life setting" (German: *Sitz im Leben*) in the
early church—in preaching, teaching, worship, and controversy—that explains why many Gospel pericopes were
preserved and recorded. Form criticism, then, though extremely subjective at times, can both clarify the process responsible for the remembering and recording of the text
and can lead to a greater appreciation of the text's life in
the experience of the early church.

   Redaction criticism is the most recent of the three subdisciplines in tradition analysis, emerging since the end of the
Second World War. The word *redaction* refers to the editorial
activity by which the evangelists utilized their sources in the
formation of our present Gospels. Redaction criticism re-
gards the writers as more than mere compilers of traditions,
but as authors in their own right. It has been shown that the
items from this tradition were selected, arranged, and presented to elucidate the theological or thematic point of view
of the individual evangelist. In reading each of the temptation accounts, for example, the interpreter discovers that
only Mark's narrative includes the detail that Jesus was
"with the wild beasts" (1:13). Mark's reference to these an-
imals may well have served to stress to his Roman audience,
some of whom at least were facing lions in the arena, that
nothing they could experience was foreign to the experience of their Lord. Many other examples of redaction criticism at work could be adduced, but what is important for
the exegete to keep in mind is that the text being studied

may exhibit editorial features that can provide clues to a deeper understanding of the passage.

Applying the Text

Besides the methods of analysis that guide us in interpreting the context and meaning of the text, special methods are required to take us from the text's message then to its significance now. However, by now it should be clear that all of the methods studied above are relevant to the task of preaching, even if they are not traditionally designated as "homiletical" in nature. For example, the more we understand the historical and literary dimensions of the text, the more the possibilities emerge for homiletics, since preaching depends to a great degree on the extent to which we are able to discern the situations today that are analogous to those addressed in the text. Likewise, grammatical exegesis is a necessary prelude to preaching in that the biblical text itself often lacks clarity, either because of variations in its transmission (the concern of textual analysis) or because of the linguistic and historical gaps between the text and the modern reader (the concerns of lexical, syntactical, structural, rhetorical, and tradition-critical analysis). Even parishioners who do not read the original languages can recognize these problems through footnotes in modern translations. Hence the more fully we are able to discern the original author's meaning, the more accurate becomes the exegetical process, and the richer the homiletical results.

It is now clear why this third aspect of exegetical understanding—that having to do with the text's significance for modern readers—is both necessary and unavoidable. Wherever the Bible is regarded as Scripture and not merely as an analyzable "object," competent exegesis is as basic to the vocation of the preacher as any other skill. As we have seen, sensitive exegesis exposes numerous ways in which preaching can bring out the meaning of the text for today. Hence the faith commitments of the exegete are not left aside in the exegetical process, but rather the reverse: since the text exists in order to speak to the community of faith, personal and other applications of the text should follow automatically.

What, then, is the role of Greek in this final step of moving from text to sermon? In my view it is essentially an advisory one. To speak of an advisory role for Greek is not to minimize the importance of the language. It rather refers to its use in providing a support base that enables the preacher to be thoroughly grounded in the historical and grammatical dimensions of the text. To borrow a thought from another New Testament teacher: "When a professor of New Testament writes about biblical preaching he is not dabbling in someone else's discipline (that of the homiletician). . . . He is simply bringing one important aspect of his work to fruition where it counts the most—or ought to."[12] In other words, New Testament exegesis is not complete until the text is applied to the present-day world—and its application to life is why the Bible was written in the first place.

This point, of course, is obvious, but it is an unfortunate fact that sermons all too frequently proceed from a cavalier handling of the biblical text, if the text is handled at all. Haddon W. Robinson has described the problem this way: "When preachers announce a text they sometimes practice sleight of mind—now you see it, now you don't. The passage and the sermon may be nothing more than strangers passing in the pulpit. Yet, it is a rape of the pulpit to ignore or avoid in the sermon what the passage teaches." Robinson's point is that faithfulness to the text is not something optional; it is an indispensable characteristic of biblical preaching. Preachers do not *make* the text relevant; they should get deep enough into the text to *find* its relevance. Thus Greek has the advantage, if the Scripture text is faithfully dealt with, of providing a biblical focus to the sermon

---

12. Leander E. Keck, *The Bible in the Pulpit: The Renewal of Biblical Preaching* (Nashville: Abingdon, 1978), p. 14.

as well as suggesting valuable hints about the shape the sermon should assume.

Conclusion

We have seen that the aim of biblical exegesis is to explain what the text meant to its original audience and what it means to hearers today. The primary exegetical principle is that the meaning of a text is the author's intended meaning, rather than "what it means to me." It is within these parameters of authorial intent and grammatical form that truly biblical interpretation takes place.

We have also seen that biblical interpretation is a rigorous activity involving questions of "context," "meaning," and "significance." The questions of context help us to situate the text within a setting chronologically far removed from our own. The object at this stage is to get a broad, panoramic view of the book within its historical and literary contexts. The questions of meaning take us through the text itself as carefully and thoroughly as possible. Here the purpose is to understand what the writer had in mind when he wrote to the original audience. Finally, the questions of significance help us to "put it all together," weighing the results of the contextual and grammatical analysis and deciding how they contribute to the overall interpretation and application of the text. The historical and literary background, the original text, the lexical meaning, the syntax, the formal structure, the rhetorical form, the tradition-history—all these deepen our understanding of the text, but they are not the goal. The goal of exegesis is to apprehend the text as a living and abiding word from God.

The purpose of this chapter was to present the most important steps involved in attaining this goal. The great variety of exegetical approaches discussed calls for three comments in conclusion. First, to this point I have not so much attempted to explain how each exegetical approach works as to bring together sometimes widely dispersed lines of research. In thus advocating a holistic approach to exegesis, I am indirectly arguing against the modern tendency toward fragmentation in the exegetical process. Each approach discussed in this chapter is but one aspect of the total range of methodologies that should be employed by the biblical student. Moreover, each type of study is most useful when it is developed and practiced with adequate reference to the canons and experience of all the other approaches. It is the task of interpretation *as a whole* that confronts us today; and part of that task is to break down the barriers that have been erected between the various methods of interpretation. To use an analogy, if three travelers were to explore the United States through different routes—one starting from California and moving eastward, another concentrating on the Pacific Northwest, and the third being confined to the eastern seaboard—they would think they were in three different countries. Multiform in every respect, the United States is nevertheless a single country. Likewise, a biblical text can be described from many different starting points, and no single way of approaching a text should ever be seen as exhausting its meaning.

In the second place, by arranging the various aspects of exegesis in the order discussed above I do not mean to suggest that the exegetical process is a mechanical succession of steps or that all the steps apply equally to all passages. Our discussion is to be understood only as portraying the overall framing logic of exegesis; in actual practice the process of exegesis may advance quite differently. For some passages the historical question will be of paramount importance, while for others the crucial matter will be lexical or syntactical. Moreover, while it may seem necessary to put "meaning" before "significance"—a principle incarnated in the *Interpreter's Bible*, which prints the "exegesis" above the "exposition"—such a neat distinction is not possible. In practice we will often find ourselves moving back and forth between interpretation and application. Indeed, the preacher who does not learn how to move in both directions is very likely to produce a sermon that imposes contemporary issues on the text or, conversely, that confuses grammatical analysis with gospel preaching. What needs to be emphasized is the necessity of going through *all* the steps so that we do not overlook any important aspect of meaning. This involves relating the various aspects of exegesis to each other, weighing the significance of each, and deciding how they contribute to the overall interpretation.

Finally, we do well to remember that exegesis is as much an art as it is a science. In interpreting the New Testament we quickly discover that there are as many answers as there are questions. This does not mean, however, that all the answers are equally correct. Exegesis demands that we work hard to safeguard the Scriptures—and ourselves—from preconceived interpretations. Our task is a kind of alchemy, transforming the walls that separate us from the text into a glass through which the text becomes clear and intelligible. To do this we need certain basic principles of interpretation that will prevent us from turning that wall of glass into a mirror in which our own reflection blots out the text. Hence, exegesis is necessary if we are to allow the text to speak for itself and avoid altering it to suit our own presuppositions.

Stop and Think

Can you briefly summarize each step of analysis discussed in this chapter and the contribution it makes to the exegetical process? Are there any steps that seem unnecessary to you? How would your approach to exegesis differ from ours?

4

Developing Your Exegetical Skills

A Concise Guide to Greek Exegesis

Bridging the gap between the ancient Greek text and the modern world has never been easy. We have seen, however, that bridge-building is both necessary and (by God's grace) possible. Now we are ready to consider the skills and techniques needed for you to take this step. Everything that was said in the preceding three chapters is only preparatory to the goal toward which we have been working. You have now prepared yourself to move with confidence and understanding into the rewarding world of Greek exegesis.

Let's see how far we have come to this point. Chapter 1 explained the need for exegesis and presented some common-sense tips for using Greek in ministry. Chapter 2 stressed the importance of building an adequate library of reference tools to help you move from text to sermon. Chapter 3 introduced the steps involved in Greek exegesis, what New Testament interpretation really requires, and, finally, the rich rewards of using Greek in your ministry.

Now the real adventure begins as we push ahead to the deeper pleasures of reading Greek with the skills and tools we have acquired. The steps given below are intended to "flesh out" the guidelines in chapter 3 and will help you not only in preaching but in personal devotion and Bible study. Each step will be discussed in greater detail in what follows, but I think a quick summary will help you see the entire process in perspective.

1. **Survey the historical context.** We must always interpret a text in light of its original historical setting. A text has no meaning—or may assume every kind of meaning—outside this parameter of historical context.
2. **Observe the larger literary context.** A survey of an entire book is necessary for the study of its individual passages. Be able to trace the development of the author's argument and show how your passage fits this context.
3. **Resolve any significant textual issues.** Important textual problems will be reflected in the major translations and in the apparatus of your Greek New Testament. Rarely, if ever, will you need to discuss such problems from the pulpit, but you should at least be certain in your own mind what the original text was.
4. **Determine the meaning of any crucial words.** Do a word study on any important terms in your passage.
5. **Analyze the syntax.** Note any syntactical features that contribute directly to the interpretation of your passage.
6. **Determine the structure.** Seek to understand the flow of the author's argument and how the major ideas in your passage are related to each other.
7. **Look for any significant rhetorical features.** New Testament authors often used various literary forms to communicate their meaning. Wherever "the medium is the message," it is of crucial importance to your exegesis to be able to show what the author was doing.

8. **Observe how any sources were used.** Look for editorial features in your passage that point to the author's distinctive literary and/or theological contributions.

9. **Determine the key thought of your passage.** Discern the life issues in your passage that have relevance to the contemporary believer. Then write down in one sentence what seems to be the central teaching of the passage.

10. **Derive a homiletical outline from the text.** Put the results of your exegesis into a workable outline that sets forth the text's claims and statements in ways that are timeless and relevant to the current needs of your congregation.

This is Greek exegesis, and it can revolutionize your life. It works—if *you* work. Master these steps and you will be able to use your Greek New Testament with skill and assurance. And you will have opened up a source of rich enjoyment for yourself.

A word of caution. Most of these steps can be mastered only when studied in concert with other areas of interpretation, including New Testament backgrounds, textual criticism, Greek syntax, and homiletics—to mention only a few of the subdisciplines involved. The following discussion is deliberately limited to the most basic guidelines, assuming on your part at least a casual acquaintance with general hermeneutical principles and a basic proficiency in translation. I have also included a bibliography of titles in the hope that you will actually *use* them.

Analyzing the Steps

Step 1. Survey the Historical Context

To begin with, become acquainted with the historical setting of the book you are studying. The key question here is, "What historical factors lie behind the writing?" You can derive much of this information from the book itself; for some of it you will need to consult various Bible study tools such as a New Testament introduction, a good commentary on the book, and a Bible dictionary (see chapter 2). Try to determine the following:

Who wrote the book?
Who were its recipients?
What kind of relationship existed between author and
    readers?
Where was the author when writing?
What situation occasioned the writing?
Is the purpose of the book explicitly stated?
Where did the readers live?
What were the recipients' special problems or needs?

The foundational assumption behind these questions is that the New Testament writings were *occasional documents*, that is, they were occasioned by some special circumstance either from the author's or the readers' perspective. The more you understand these circumstances, the better you will be able to apply the biblical message to modern life.

On historical backgrounds, the following resources will be especially helpful:

Frederick F. Bruce. *New Testament History*. Garden City, N.Y.: Doubleday, 1971.

Charles K. Barrett. *The New Testament Background: Selected Documents*. Revised edition. San Francisco: Harper/ London: SPCK, 1987.

Everett Ferguson. *Backgrounds of Early Christianity*. Grand Rapids: Eerdmans, 1987.

David E. Garland. "Background Studies and New Testament Interpretation." Pp. 349–76 in *New Testament Criticism and Interpretation*. Edited by David Alan Black and David S. Dockery. Grand Rapids: Zondervan, 1991.

Step 2. Observe the Larger Literary Context

The second step is based on two assumptions. First, the basic unit of exegesis is the paragraph—a distinct group of sentences with a single theme. Second, thought is usually expressed in a series of related ideas. A New Testament writing is not an accidental junk pile of miscellaneous elements. Instead it is like a jigsaw puzzle, where each piece fits into those that surround it, and where an isolated piece cannot make sense when removed from its proper place in the overall pattern. Seeing this pattern will keep you from distorting the parts that make up the whole.

Begin by establishing the genre of the whole book of which your passage is a part. The four basic genres in the New Testament are Gospel, Acts, Epistle, and Apocalypse. Within each type are subtypes such as narrative, miracle story, parable, wisdom saying, hymn, exhortation, quotation, prophecy, beatitude, and so forth. The New Testament literary forms affect our understanding of the text in much the same way as differences between feature stories, editorials, and obituaries influence our reading of newspapers today. It is therefore *crucial* to determine the genre(s) you are dealing with before attempting to discern the meaning of your passage.

After you have established the type of literature you are dealing with, get acquainted with the outline of the book in which your passage is found. Try to set aside a block of time to read the entire book in one sitting without interruptions. Do your best to divide the book into its proper subsections, that is, the teaching blocks that reflect what the writer has said on his theme. Then determine the limits of your preaching text by observing both its *syntax* and *subject matter*. Pay special attention to the connectives (conjunctions and particles). Look for words such as "therefore," "so then," "for this reason," and "because of this." These are not the only words that indicate the beginning of a new paragraph, but they almost always do. Commentaries and New Testament surveys should also be consulted at this point. Finally, it may be helpful to check the paragraphing in your Greek New Testament against two or more modern translations (e.g., NIV, NRSV, REB). If necessary, adjust (enlarge or shorten) your preaching text to conform to the natural boundaries indicated in the text itself.

For an excellent overview of the New Testament genres, you may wish to consult the following:

> Craig L. Blomberg. "The Diversity of Literary Genres in the New Testament." Pp. 507–32 in *New Testament Criticism and Interpretation*. Edited by David Alan Black and David S. Dockery. Grand Rapids: Zondervan, 1991.

The attempt to discern the internal unity and structure of a writing is called discourse analysis. For an introduction to this field of study, see the following:

> David Alan Black (ed.). *Linguistics and New Testament Interpretation: Essays on Discourse Analysis*. Nashville: Broadman, 1993.

Step 3. Resolve Any Significant Textual Issues

The overwhelming majority of variants between the Greek manuscripts of the New Testament are of minor importance. Significant variants number around two thousand. The majority of these are carefully discussed in Bruce M. Metzger's *Textual Commentary*, an indispensable resource for New Testament students (see the discussion in chapter 2). If there are any alternative textual readings in your passage that affect the meaning of the text, you will need to examine the evidence in support of each reading. Both external and internal evidence should be weighed. The questions of external evidence include the following:

Which reading is the oldest?
Which reading has wider geographical distribution?

Which reading is supported by several text types?

The questions of internal evidence include the following:

Which reading best explains the origin of the others?
Which reading can be attributed to scribal error?
Which reading best conforms to the author's style and
   thought?

Because textual criticism deals with various kinds of errors in the existing Greek manuscripts, it is necessary to
know something about the types of errors that occur. The
two basic categories of errors are *accidental* and *intentional*.
Accidental errors often resulted from the text being read
aloud and scribes relying on their hearing to record the text
(see Rom. 5:1, where the manuscripts are divided between
εἰρήνην ἔχομεν [we have peace] and εἰρήνην ἔχωμεν [let us
have peace]). Other types of accidental errors include those
stemming from misunderstanding or forgetfulness (e.g.,
changes in word order, the substitution of synonyms, the
unintentional harmonization of similar passages, etc.). Intentional errors include changes to correct an apparent
error of fact (see Mark 1:2), harmonization of parallel passages (see Luke 11:2–4), and doctrinal corrections (see
Rom. 8:1).

In order to do your own textual criticism, you will need
a working knowledge of the materials used in determining
the original text (i.e., Greek manuscripts, ancient versions,
and citations by early church fathers), a familiarity with the
textual apparatus of your Greek New Testament, and an
understanding of how textual decisions are made. These
matters need not be discussed here as they are thoroughly
treated elsewhere. For an overview of the main issues related to New Testament textual criticism, you should read
at least one of the following:

Bruce M. Metzger. "Introduction." Pp. xiii–xxxi in *A Textual Commentary on the Greek New Testament*. New York/London: United Bible Societies, 1971.

Gordon D. Fee. "The Textual Criticism of the New Testament." Pp. 419–33 in *The Expositor's Bible Commentary*, vol. 1. Edited by Frank E. Gaebelein. Grand Rapids: Zondervan, 1979.

Michael W. Holmes. "Textual Criticism." Pp. 101–34 in *New Testament Criticism and Interpretation*. Edited by David Alan Black and David S. Dockery. Grand Rapids: Zondervan, 1991.

David Alan Black. "New Testament Textual Criticism." In *Holman Bible Introduction*. Edited by David S. Dockery et al. Nashville: Broadman, forthcoming.

If you have time, also look at one of the standard introductions mentioned in chapter 2 (i.e., Metzger's *Text of the New Testament* or Greenlee's *Introduction to New Testament Textual Criticism*).

Step 4. Determine the Meaning of Any Crucial Words

Words are always important because they are the basic building blocks of language. Some passages will contain words whose meaning is either unclear, ambiguous, or theologically important. If you feel that your understanding of such words is inadequate, you can profit from doing a word study. As a rule, each word has several meanings. But under normal circumstances, that word has only one meaning in its context. Therefore, our responsibility is to discern the meaning that the author intended. For each word, ask the following questions:

What are its possible meanings?
Which meaning best fits this context?
How is the word used by the same author in other passages?

Does the word have any special connotative meaning
(e.g., leper, Samaritan, slave)?
Are there any synonyms or opposites in the context that
can help to define its meaning?

Be aware of the following fallacies:

Etymologizing (determining meaning solely on the basis
of a word's etymology).
Illegitimate totality transfer (reading the full range of
meanings that a word may have into each context in
which it occurs).
Confusing word with concept (failing to recognize that
ideas are rarely expressed at the word level alone).
Over-analysis (performing word studies to the neglect of
other areas of exegesis).

These fallacies are easy to commit and are very "preach-
able," but they are to be avoided at all costs. Preachers who
love to talk about the "real" meaning of a Greek word are
usually etymologizing. The key to lexical analysis is to remember that a word can have several meanings, only one
of which is likely to be its semantic contribution to any particular sentence in which it occurs. For most words, I recommend the following procedure. First, consult the major
lexicons (especially BAGD and Louw and Nida's *Lexicon*) to
get an idea of the range of meaning of a word you are studying. Next, check a concordance to get a feel for your author's distinctive use of the term. Finally, if you sense that
a word needs additional study, look it up in *NIDNTT*.
The following books will help you develop your skills in
doing word studies:

Moisés Silva. *Biblical Words and Their Meaning: An Introduc-
tion to Lexical Semantics.* Grand Rapids: Zondervan, 1983.
Donald A. Carson. *Exegetical Fallacies.* Grand Rapids:
Baker, 1984 (esp. chap. 1: "Word Study Fallacies").

David Alan Black. *Linguistics for Students of New Testament Greek: A Survey of Basic Concepts and Applications.* Grand Rapids: Baker, 1988 (esp. chap. 5: "Semantics: Determining Meaning").

Neal Windham. *New Testament Greek for Preachers and Teachers.* Lanham, Md.: University Press of America, 1991 (esp. chap. 5: "Words and Phrases: Determining the Meaning of New Testament Vocabulary").

Step 5. Analyze the Syntax

Syntax involves the grammatical and semantic relationships that exist between words. The study of syntax will inevitably take you back to the Greek text. Through the reading of commentaries you will also be alerted to further questions that need to be considered. Your primary concern in syntactical analysis is to isolate any grammatical feature that might affect your interpretation of the passage. Areas of importance for exegesis include the following:

The presence or absence of the definite article.
The tense (aspect) and voice of verbal forms.
The case of nouns and pronouns.
Word, phrase, and clause order.
Prepositions.
Conjunctions.

When you encounter questions of syntax, you will want to consult BDF along with one or several of the following standard textbooks:

James A. Brooks and Carlton L. Winbery. *Syntax of New Testament Greek.* Lanham, Md.: University Press of America, 1979.

H. E. Dana and Julius R. Mantey. *A Manual Grammar of New Testament Greek.* New York: Macmillan, 1927.

J. Harold Greenlee. *A Concise Exegetical Grammar of New Testament Greek*. 5th edition. Grand Rapids: Eerdmans, 1986.

A more complete discussion of verbal aspect and of word, phrase, and clause order may be found in the following:

David Alan Black. *Learn to Read New Testament Greek*. Nashville: Broadman, 1993 (esp. chap. 26: "Reading Your Greek New Testament: Six Areas of Application").

Step 6. Determine the Structure

Structural analysis is concerned with the relationships that exist between larger units of meaning such as clauses and sentences. For complex passages, it will be helpful to make a full structural analysis at this point. The aim of a structural analysis is to rearrange the words of a passage in such a way that the central theme of the text becomes evident. The analysis will also reveal the relationships that exist between the main clause and any dependent clauses that may be present in the text. The main clause will normally indicate the main proposition (idea) of the text, while the dependent clauses generally represent expansions of the main idea. One word of caution is in order: what may appear as a main clause in English is often a dependent clause in Greek. It is therefore necessary to work from the Greek text as much as possible when doing a structural analysis.

There is no "correct" way to analyze a passage, nor is there a set pattern or procedure in this method of study. You should develop the kind of procedure that best suits your needs and desires. The procedure I prefer to follow consists of three basic steps:

1. Place all independent clauses at the left-hand margin of the page.

2. Place all dependent clauses or phrases on the next line under the word(s) they modify.
3. Restate the author's argument in your own words.

At this point you are "charting" the passage, seeking to draw the parts into a whole and relating them to one another. Again, the object is to reconstruct as clearly as possible the original thought of the author. The following is a sample analysis taken from Philippians 1:9–11:

And this is my prayer [τοῦτο προσεύχομαι]
   that [ἵνα] your love may abound still more and more
   with knowledge and discernment
      in order that you may approve [εἰς τὸ δοκιμάζειν ὑμᾶς]
      what is excellent
         so that [ἵνα] you may be pure and blameless in the
         day of Christ
            having been filled [πεπληρωμένοι] with the fruit
            of righteousness
               that comes through Jesus Christ
               to the glory and praise of God

The flow of thought as diagrammed above may be expressed as follows:

My prayer is that your love for one another may overflow with knowledge and full insight. The purpose of such discerning love is to help you determine what is best, so that when Christ returns you may be pure and blameless. Such holy living is only possible because you have already been filled with the righteousness of God through Jesus Christ. God has done this in order that he might bring honor and glory to himself.

This type of analysis maximizes your opportunity to be truly inductive in your Bible study. For this reason, the study of structure is for many expositors the most enjoyable and rewarding aspect of their work in the Greek text. It is one of the most effective ways of grasping the argument of your passage.

Following the analysis, you may construct an outline based on its main features (see step 10). Where there is uncertainty as to the author's argument, consult the commentaries and other English versions. Above all, never make a decision on the basis of what you would like the passage to say. Seek to be faithful to the way in which the Holy Spirit structured the original text.

For more help on sentence diagramming, see the following:

> Johannes P. Louw. *Semantics of New Testament Greek.* Philadelphia: Fortress/Chico, Calif.: Scholars Press, 1982 (pp. 67–158).
> Gordon D. Fee. *New Testament Exegesis: A Handbook for Students and Pastors.* Philadelphia: Westminster, 1983 (pp. 60–77).
> Walter L. Liefeld. *New Testament Exposition: From Text to Sermon.* Grand Rapids: Zondervan, 1984 (pp. 45–56).

Step 7. Look for Any Significant Rhetorical Features

How something is said is often as important as *what* is said. Therefore, as you study your passage, you will also want to become aware of its literary form. The text's design is part of its meaning, and to neglect this design is somewhat like covering a great cathedral with plywood siding. Some things to look for as you analyze style are the following:

Alliteration (the repetition of words beginning with the same letter or sound).
Asyndeton (the omission of conjunctions that would normally be present).
Chiasmus (the rhetorical inversion of words or thoughts).
Paronomasia (an intentional play on two similar-sounding words).
Polysyndeton (the superfluous repetition of conjunctions).

The observations you make in this stage will vary in length, depending on how much time you are able to give to the study. Don't become discouraged if you don't observe much the first few times you look for rhetorical forms. With practice your observations will increase both in number and depth. You may wish to secure and read the following:

Eugene A. Nida, Johannes P. Louw, A. H. Snyman, and J. v. W. Cronjé. *Style and Discourse, with Special Reference to the Text of the Greek New Testament*. Cape Town: Bible Society of South Africa, 1983.

David Alan Black. *Linguistics for Students of New Testament Greek: A Survey of Basic Concepts and Applications*. Grand Rapids: Baker, 1988 (pp. 132–36; much of the material in Nida's book has been summarized in my volume).

Step 8. Observe How Any Sources Were Used

Do not spend a lot of time trying to isolate the sources behind a particular book or passage; your focus must always be on the final form of the text. The important thing to note at this stage is that in the Gospels (and to a lesser extent in the other New Testament writings) different writers treat the same traditions in different ways. If you are studying a Gospel text it is helpful to consult a synopsis. Try to determine how the passage contributes to the evangelist's life setting. Once you know how your text functioned in its own life setting, you will find the relationship between the body of your sermon and its conclusion less disjunctive.

For more information on tradition analysis, see the following:

Scot McKnight. *Interpreting the Synoptic Gospels*. Guides to New Testament Exegesis 2. Grand Rapids: Baker, 1988.

Grant R. Osborne. "Redaction Criticism." Pp. 199–224 in *New Testament Criticism and Interpretation*. Edited by

David Alan Black and David S. Dockery. Grand Rapids: Zondervan, 1991.

Step 9. Determine the Key Thought of Your Passage

In the next step you begin to focus directly on application. On a sheet of paper, list the main ideas of the passage. Then look for the pivotal idea that is amplified in some respect in the rest of the passage. This is the *key thought* of the passage. This thought should be developed as the primary truth of your passage. Generally speaking, there is only one key thought to a passage, not several. This truth may be verbalized in various ways, but the core will remain the same.

For example, Paul's admonition to Euodia and Syntyche to live harmoniously (Phil. 4:2) was originally addressed to the Philippians. The meaning of the passage can be stated in this way: "Euodia and Syntyche are to stop quarreling and are to live harmoniously in the Lord." But the underlying principle is relevant to every Christian in all cultures everywhere. The obvious principle deduced from the passage is simply this: "Christians who are quarreling must stop it and should live harmoniously." This principle—that believers should live in harmony with one another—is as valid today as it was in the days of the Philippians.

This stage of analysis is the "meat and potatoes" of your study of Scripture. As the years go by, you will lean on it as the mainstay in your sermon preparation, for the application of truth is *the* major need in churches today. Let us keep in mind that the New Testament was not written primarily for our information, but for our transformation. Therefore, we must take the time to think through the life-changing truth of the text.

Step 10. Derive a Homiletical Outline from the Text

You are now ready to pass on to others what you have had the privilege of learning (2 Tim. 2:2). Reduced to its simplest terms, the development of a sermon involves two basic activities: the determining of the biblical message to be proclaimed (step 9) and the arranging of that message into a coherent sermonic structure (step 10). The goal is to achieve unity between message and structure. As much as possible, the design of your sermon should be quarried from the biblical text itself, hewn and chiseled to proper proportions to produce a strong and beautiful structure.

Begin by determining what you think to be the central teaching of your passage (see step 9), and state it in your own words in a complete sentence. This statement must be definite, precise, and faithful to the intent of the original author. Then gather the supporting points that bear on this central teaching, and list them in a logical sequence. Remember that both the *shape* and the *content* of your message should arise from the passage itself. Be sure to construct your homiletical outline in such a fashion that the listeners can follow the sermon in their own Bibles. Produce a title for the sermon and for the various divisions of your sermon. Finally, write several paragraphs (including illustrations) elaborating on the central truth of the text.

For helpful guides on this step of exegesis, see the following:

Haddon W. Robinson. *Biblical Preaching: The Development and Delivery of Expository Messages*. Grand Rapids: Baker, 1980.

John R. W. Stott. *Between Two Worlds: The Art of Preaching in the Twentieth Century*. Grand Rapids: Eerdmans, 1982.

Walter L. Liefeld. *New Testament Exposition: From Text to Sermon*. Grand Rapids: Zondervan, 1984.

These, then, are the steps needed to go from text to sermon. As you begin this process, don't be intimidated by the newness of the approach or the variety of methods. Select your own level of difficulty, adding various steps as you become increasingly proficient in them. The steps do not have to be done in the precise order presented above (though steps 1–8 must be done before steps 9–10); you may adjust the method to your own priorities and time constraints.

You will also need to weigh carefully how much original research you should do. Only you can determine whether you will diagram a passage or look up a word in *NIDNTT*. My advice is to try your hand at each step, but to concentrate on the historical and literary contexts (steps 1–2), on the syntactical structure (steps 5–6), and on producing a homiletical outline that is faithful to the original author's intent (steps 9–10). Whenever a passage is studied with these key factors in operation, the chances are good that an informed understanding of the text will be the result.

Above all, keep in mind that a truly biblical sermon never goes beyond the original meaning and function of the text. This does not mean that you cannot emphasize dimensions of the text that seem to bear on the modern situation. Like an orchestra conductor, you may choose to highlight or modify themes for a particular occasion. Nevertheless, whether your sermon explicitly unfolds the text or only alludes to it, you should practice responsible exegesis.

Applying the Steps: 1 Thessalonians 5:16–18

If you feel comfortable with these steps and want to proceed further, you might want to study this passage on your own before comparing the results of your exegesis with mine. For purposes of illustration, suppose that you have been asked to speak on 1 Thessalonians 5:16–18: "Rejoice always, pray without ceasing, give thanks in all circumstances; for this is the will of God in Christ Jesus for you" (NRSV).

Step 1. Survey the Historical Context

Begin with the book of 1 Thessalonians itself. Note any and every detail that throws light on the historical situation between Paul and the Thessalonian believers. Your summary may look something like this:

First Thessalonians was written almost immediately after Paul's sudden departure from Thessalonica. Yet the hostility that had driven Paul from the city continued, and some of the Thessalonian converts were on the verge of losing all hope. Moreover, certain carnal tendencies were developing in the church: immorality (4:3–8), idleness (4:9–12), and disunity (5:12–13). These babes in Christ needed encouragement!

At this point any good Bible dictionary article on "Thessalonica" can provide additional details about the cultural, political, and religious background of the city in which the church was found. Biblical commentaries often provide such useful information.

Step 2. Observe the Larger Literary Context

Most interpreters agree that 1 Thessalonians has two main divisions: commendation (1:2–3:13) and correction (4:1–5:22). On the one hand, Paul is encouraged that the Thessalonians have remained faithful to Christ despite severe persecution (3:8); on the other hand, he is deeply concerned about certain areas where they are "lacking in faith" (3:10).

The triad of exhortations in 5:16–18 is found in this second part of the letter, particularly in the section comprising 5:12–22. In these verses Paul is urging the Thessalonians on to deeper spirituality. The exhortations in 5:12–22 are headed by a list of injunctions regarding proper attitudes toward leaders (vv. 12–13) and toward the whole church (vv. 14–15). Paul's command to be joyful, prayerful, and thankful is closely related to these verses. There can be no compliance with the regulations in verses 12–15 apart from constant communion with God (vv. 16–18). In other words, if we are inwardly contaminated, fulfilling God's will toward others is impossible. Hence in verses 16–18 Paul turns to the believer's inner life.

Step 3. Resolve Any Significant Textual Issues

A glance at the textual apparatus of *GNT* or at Metzger's *Textual Commentary* reveals that no textual variation exists in these verses, so we can move on to the next step.

Step 4. Determine the Meaning of Any Crucial Words

In 1 Thessalonians 5:16–18 the pivotal words are clearly the verbs "rejoice," "pray," and "give thanks." The following is a sample list of observations gleaned from BAGD and Louw and Nida's *Lexicon*:

χαίρετε (rejoice) differs from both εὐφραίνομαι (I rejoice as an expression of happiness) and συνήδομαι (I rejoice as a result of some pleasurable experience). Apparently Paul envisions a joy that is independent of one's circumstances.

προσεύχεσθε (pray) is a comprehensive term, expressing prayer generally, in contrast to δέομαι, which focuses on specific prayers for specific needs. Petition is indeed an important aspect of prayer (see 3:10), but the term Paul uses here is broad enough to include other forms of prayer as well (e.g., thanksgiving, v. 18).

εὐχαριστεῖτε (give thanks) is the primary term for thanksgiving in the New Testament. It is almost always used for thanksgiving to God, not to people. The verb is found in the words of the institution of the Lord's Supper; hence the name "Eucharist."

Step 5. Analyze the Syntax

Your list of significant syntactical points might look something like this:

All three verbs are in the imperative mood, showing that rejoicing, praying, and giving thanks are not options but requirements.

All three verbs are in the present tense, implying that rejoicing, praying, and giving thanks are to be constant
and habitual activities.

Although "this" (τοῦτο) in verse 18 is singular, it probably
applies to all three commands. In other words, they represent three aspects of one attitude, not three different
attitudes to life. All three must be practiced together.

ἐν παντί (v. 18) does not mean "at every time" (as does πάντοτε in v. 16) but "in everything," that is, in every circumstance. Paul does not say to be thankful *for*
everything, but *in* everything.

Paul uses the word "will" (θέλημα) without the definite
article. This seems to imply that he is not attempting to
describe *the* whole will of God, but rather some aspect
of it. God's will includes many other things of importance (see 4:3).

The phrase ἐν Χριστῷ (v. 18) is a classic Pauline expression, emphasizing the centrality of Christ in all the believer does. We cannot know what God wants for us
apart from his revealed will in Christ, nor can we carry
out that will apart from Christ's enabling presence.

Step 6. Determine the Structure

The structure of these verses is quite simple. Paul lists
three activities that should characterize the Christian, then
he grounds his commands in the will of God in Christ Jesus:

v. 16	rejoice	
v. 17	pray	} the will of God in Christ Jesus
v. 18	give thanks	

The flow of thought may be summarized as follows: "An in-
tegral part of Christian living is being joyful, prayerful, and
thankful. This is what God wants from those who have put
their faith in Christ."

Step 7. Look for Any Significant Rhetorical Features

Rhetorical features in 1 Thessalonians 5:16–18 include the following:

Alliteration with π: πάντοτε . . . προσεύχεσθε . . . πάντι. This feature delights the ear and provides points of contact between the verses.

Asyndeton (the absence of conjunctions between vv. 16–18). The author repeatedly stabs our ears with a rapid barrage of spiritual requirements.

Chiasmus (this type of structure often calls attention to the middle element, here, the believer's obligation to pray without ceasing):

A π<u>άν</u>τοτε (v. 16)
B   προσεύχεσθε (v. 17)
A´ ἐν π<u>άν</u>τι (v. 18)

The "rule of three": (1) rejoice, (2) pray, (3) give thanks. This triad gives the text a feeling of balance and cohesiveness. The triadic arrangement of words and phrases is remarkably frequent in 1 Thessalonians (see 1:3; 2:10, 19; 5:8, 23).

Step 8. Observe How Any Sources Were Used

The injunction to continual prayer springs from the same idea expressed in Luke 18:1–8 in the parable of the unjust judge (if a dishonest judge yields to the persistent cries of a widow, how much more will the upright God and Father of us all!). This theme is also very similar to that of the parable of the persistent friend in Luke 11:5–8. Clearly, persistent prayer was an important teaching of our Lord himself!

Step 9. Determine the Key Thought of Your Passage

Tie the verses together into one "big idea." In one sentence write the distilled essence or theme of the passage: "God wants us to be constantly joyful, prayerful, and thankful."

Step 10. Derive a Homiletical Outline from the Text

The goal in the final step is to take the key thought and relate it both to the historical situation reflected in the book and to the life issues facing modern believers. Since worry in the midst of life's difficulties was a major problem among the Thessalonians, and since Paul seems to be addressing this problem by focusing on the alternatives to worry (i.e., joy, prayer, and thankfulness), this issue has been incorporated into the following homiletical outline and summary (under each of the three main points of the body, I have included appropriate illustrations):

Title: God's Plan for Winning over Worry

Theme: God wants us to win over worry by being joyful, prayerful, and thankful

Outline: I. Introduction: What is God's will for us in the midst of life's worries?

II. Body
  A. That we be joyful
  B. That we be prayerful
  C. That we be thankful

III. Conclusion: Paul's formula for victory over worry

Sermon summary: The Thessalonian believers were saddled with worries and cares. Recent converts to Christ, they were unprepared for the severe testing they had experienced after Paul's sudden departure from Thessalonica. Huddled together in Jason's home, they open Paul's letter to them. The apostle has many words of praise, but he also has some concerns. In the midst of life's difficulties, says Paul, it is all too easy to lose one's joy and hope. Does God have anything to say in such a situation?

Here in 1 Thessalonians 5:16–18, Paul says that believers can be victorious over worry through being joyful, prayerful, and thankful—regardless of their circumstances. The first of his commands, "rejoice always" (v. 16), is especially linked to what he has been saying in verse 15: When wronged, we must refuse to nurse a grudge or to retaliate. Our joy is not dependent on favorable circumstances or on how we are treated by others. Suffering is the rule of Christian living (3:1–5), but we need not allow anything to disturb our composure. We can have a song in our hearts because we are "in Christ" and enjoy the fruit of his Spirit (Gal. 5:22). [Illustration: the persecution and poverty of the Thessalonians. They thought more about Christ than about their earthly difficulties (1:6).]

Paul's next command—"pray without ceasing" (v. 17)—springs from the same idea as that behind his command to be constantly joyful. Rejoicing in Christ regardless of our circumstances reminds us that we can turn to him at any time for help in our daily walk. Prayer is the chief expression of this dependent attitude. In his book *Knowing God*, James I. Packer says that people who know God are, above all, people of prayer.[1] Prayer, however, is not only asking God for things. The word Paul uses here for prayer expresses general devotion, a Godward attitude. True prayer focuses on God and his sufficiency, not on our needs. Though it is impossible for us always to be uttering words of prayer, we can and should always live in this spirit of prayer. [Illustration: Paul often broke out in spontaneous prayer, even when writing his letters (this is especially true in these two letters to the Thessalonians). Prayer was as natural for Paul as breathing. Time and again his spirit of prayer overflowed into uttered prayer.]

Paul completes his trio of spiritual characteristics with the command: "give thanks in all circumstances" (v. 18). Like the preceding two, this command flows from the great central truth of being "in Christ." When we were in the world, life was but a matter of chance. But when we came to be "in Christ," all that changed. Now we know that, even in the

1. J. I. Packer, *Knowing God* (Downers Grove, Ill.: InterVarsity, 1973).

most difficult circumstances, God's loving purpose for our lives is being worked out. When we realize this, we can begin to give thanks in (though not necessarily *for*) every circumstance of life. [Illustration: Paul had much to be grateful for, and he often expressed that thankfulness in prayer. For example, he was constantly grateful to God for the Thessalonians (see 1:2: "We *always* thank God for all of you").]

Each of these qualities—joyfulness, prayerfulness, and thankfulness—is the will of God for us (v. 18). They are not merely suggestions made by Paul, but divine requirements. For Paul, praise, prayer, and appreciation are required just as much as proper ethical behavior. Moreover, there is never a time when we should not be joyful, prayerful, or thankful. The challenge is to make these attitudes *consistent*!

In conclusion, Paul is telling us that there is indeed a solution for fretting and stewing over our problems. Here is his formula for victory over worry: *Praise* plus *prayer* plus *appreciation* equals *peace*. Observance of this formula can sweeten our spirits and give meaning and purpose to our lives. Praise means rejoicing in who God is and in what he is doing in our lives. Prayer means living in the constant and conscious awareness of his presence, purpose, and power. Appreciation means being thankful to God that he is in control of our lives and is working out everything for our good and his glory. Remember the formula: praise plus prayer plus appreciation equals peace. [If I were preaching from this passage, I would place this formula in the Sunday worship guide, written in large letters on an insert. I would then suggest that the audience take it out and place it where they will see it every day—on the bathroom mirror or office desk. In addition, I would further suggest that they memorize the verses found in 1 Thessalonians 5:16–18, repeating them every morning and every night until they are firmly committed to memory. Then the next time worry traps them and they don't know where to turn, hopefully they will talk to the Lord about it and give him a chance to help. They will rejoice that he is their friend and thank him that he is bigger than their problems. And they will be well on their way to the conquest of worry.]

Conclusion

It remains simply to say that what I have offered in this chapter is nothing more than the reflections of one who is more anxious to learn from his fellow preachers than to teach them. My own habit is to go through these steps somewhat mechanically from beginning to end. This, for me, means about eight to ten hours of reading and reflection, but how much time is needed to go from background analysis to homiletical outline will vary from preacher to preacher. The Spirit works sovereignly, and, when all is said and done, we must place all our preparations in his hands.

Stop and Think

How would you go about exegeting 1 Thessalonians 5:16–18? Is there anything in my analysis that seems unclear, irrelevant, or forced? Do you now feel better able to exegete a text on your own?

From Theory to Practice

Employing the Principles and Tools

The following sample is taken from Philippians 2:1–4, a call to unity and humility in the face of factiousness and strife. Working through this passage will help you improve the skills you have acquired and will launch you into developing your own method of doing exegesis. You may record your thoughts in the spaces provided below.

In developing the exegesis of this text, use your Greek New Testament as much as possible, but do not hesitate to consult other tools, including concordances, commentaries, and grammars. It is particularly helpful to notice the text's literary form, since the passage is very carefully constructed. In a brief essay entitled "Paul and Christian Unity: A Formal Analysis of Philippians 2:1–4,"[1] I have attempted to shed some light on the form of the passage, as has Moisés Silva in his recent commentary on Philippians.[2] On questions of historical context, I have found Gerald F. Hawthorne's vol-

1. *Journal of the Evangelical Theological Society* 28 (1985), pp. 299–308.
2. Moisés Silva, *Philippians* (Baker Exegetical Commentary on the New Testament; Grand Rapids: Baker, 1992), pp. 99–104.

ume on Philippians in the Word Biblical Commentary to be especially illuminating.[3] The better you know the world of the original readers, the better you can illustrate and apply your message. To preach from this text also requires careful attention to the dominant thought of the passage. We need to ask, "What truth about God and about his saving work in our lives is described in this passage?" When we can answer that question, we are on firm ground to preach from this text. My hope is that this exercise will help you develop your own philosophy of expository preaching in your role as an interpreter of God's Word to God's people.

At this point, I am saying goodbye to you as you set out on an adventure that never ends. Your progress has brought you to the gateway of the challenging yet rewarding world of preaching from the New Testament. Enjoy it!

Step 1. Survey the Historical Context

Step 2. Observe the Larger Literary Context

3. Gerald F. Hawthorne, *Philippians* (Word Biblical Commentary 43; Waco, Tex.: Word, 1983).

Step 3. Resolve Any Significant Textual Issues

Step 4. Determine the Meaning of Any Crucial Words

Step 5. Analyze the Syntax

Step 6. Determine the Structure

Step 7. Look for Any Significant Rhetorical Features

Step 8. Observe How Any Sources Were Used

Step 9. Determine the Key Thought of Your Passage

Step 10. Derive a Homiletical Outline from the Text

Bibliography

This bibliography contains full publication data for the items listed in chapter 2 (excluding Bible versions).

Abbott-Smith, George. *A Manual Greek Lexicon of the New Testament.* New York: Scribner/Edinburgh: T. & T. Clark, 1921.

Aland, Kurt (ed.). *Synopsis of the Four Gospels.* 4th/5th edition. [New York:] United Bible Societies, 1982.

———. *Synopsis Quattuor Evangeliorum.* 13th edition. Stuttgart: Württembergische Bibelanstalt, 1985 (3d corrected printing in 1988).

Aland, Kurt, and Barbara Aland (eds.). *Greek-English New Testament.* 5th edition. Stuttgart: Deutsche Bibelgesellschaft, 1990.

Aland, Kurt, Matthew Black, Carlo M. Martini, Bruce M. Metzger, and Allen Wikgren (eds.). *The Greek New Testament.* 3d (corrected) edition. [New York:] United Bible Societies, 1983.

Bachmann, Horst, and Wolfgang A. Slaby (eds.). *Computer-Konkordanz zum Novum Testamentum Graece.* Berlin/New York: de Gruyter, 1980.

Bauer, Walter. *A Greek-English Lexicon of the New Testament and Other Early Christian Literature.* Translated and adapted by William F. Arndt and F. Wilbur Gingrich. 2d English edition revised by F. Wilbur Gingrich and Frederick W. Danker. Chicago: University of Chicago Press, 1979.

Berry, George R. *Interlinear Greek-English New Testament.* Reprinted Grand Rapids: Baker, 1992.

Black, David Alan. *Linguistics for Students of New Testament Greek: A Survey of Basic Concepts and Applications.* Grand Rapids: Baker, 1988.

Black, David Alan, and David S. Dockery (eds.). *New Testament Criticism and Interpretation.* Grand Rapids: Zondervan, 1991.

Blass, Friedrich, and Albert Debrunner. *A Greek Grammar of the New Testament and Other Early Christian Literature*. Translated by Robert W. Funk. Chicago: University of Chicago Press, 1961.

Bromiley, Geoffrey W. (ed.). *The International Standard Bible Encyclopedia*. Revised edition. 4 vols. Grand Rapids: Eerdmans, 1979–88.

Brown, Colin (ed.). *The New International Dictionary of New Testament Theology*. 4 vols. Grand Rapids: Zondervan, 1975–86.

Bruce, F. F. *New Testament History*. Garden City, N.Y.: Doubleday, 1971.

Chapman, Benjamin. *Greek New Testament Insert*. Grand Rapids: Baker, 1978.

Cotterell, Peter, and Max Turner. *Linguistics and Biblical Interpretation*. Downers Grove, Ill.: InterVarsity, 1989.

Dana, H. E., and Julius R. Mantey. *A Manual Grammar of the Greek New Testament*. New York: Macmillan, 1927.

The Eight Translation New Testament. Wheaton, Ill.: Tyndale, 1974.

Greenlee, J. Harold. *Introduction to New Testament Textual Criticism*. Grand Rapids: Eerdmans, 1964.

Guillemette, Pierre. *The Greek New Testament Analyzed*. Scottdale, Pa.: Herald, 1986.

Gundry, Robert H. *A Survey of the New Testament*. Grand Rapids: Zondervan, 1981.

Guthrie, Donald. *New Testament Introduction*. Downers Grove, Ill.: InterVarsity, 1965.

————. *New Testament Theology*. Downers Grove, Ill.: InterVarsity, 1981.

Harrison, Everett F. *Introduction to the New Testament*. 2d edition. Grand Rapids: Eerdmans, 1971.

Hasel, Gerhard F. *New Testament Theology: Basic Issues in the Current Debate*. Grand Rapids: Eerdmans, 1978.

Hort, Erasmus. *The Bible Book: Resources for Reading the New Testament*. New York: Crossroad, 1983.

Kittel, Gerhard, and Gerhard Friedrich (eds.). *Theological Dictionary of the New Testament*. Translated and edited by Geoffrey W. Bromiley. 10 vols. Grand Rapids: Eerdmans, 1964–76.

————. *Theological Dictionary of the New Testament*. Translated and edited by Geoffrey W. Bromiley. Abridged in 1 vol. by Geoffrey W. Bromiley. Grand Rapids: Eerdmans, 1985.

Ladd, George E. *A Theology of the New Testament*. Grand Rapids: Eerdmans, 1974.

Louw, Johannes P. *Semantics of New Testament Greek*. Philadelphia: Fortress/Chico, Calif.: Scholars Press, 1982.

Louw, Johannes P., and Eugene A. Nida. *Greek-English Lexicon of the New Testament Based on Semantic Domains*. 2 vols. New York: United Bible Societies, 1988.

Marshall, Alfred. *The NASB Interlinear Greek English New Testament*. Grand Rapids: Zondervan, 1984.

―――. *The NRSV-NIV Parallel New Testament in Greek and English, with an Interlinear Translation*. Grand Rapids: Zondervan, 1990.

Marshall, I. Howard (ed.). *New Testament Interpretation: Essays on Principles and Methods*. Grand Rapids: Eerdmans, 1977.

Martin, Ralph P. *New Testament Books for Pastor and Teacher*. Philadelphia: Westminster, 1984.

―――. *New Testament Foundations: A Guide for Christian Students*. 2 vols. Grand Rapids: Eerdmans, 1978.

Metzger, Bruce M. *Lexical Aids for Students of New Testament Greek*. Princeton: Theological Book Agency, 1969.

―――. *The Text of the New Testament*. 3d edition. Oxford: Oxford University Press, 1992.

―――. *A Textual Commentary on the Greek New Testament*. Corrected edition. New York/London: United Bible Societies, 1975.

Morris, Leon. *New Testament Theology*. Grand Rapids: Zondervan, 1986.

Moule, C. F. D. *An Idiom Book of New Testament Greek*. 2d edition. Cambridge: Cambridge University Press, 1959.

Moulton, James H., Wilbert F. Howard, and Nigel Turner. *A Grammar of New Testament Greek*. 4 vols. Edinburgh: T. & T. Clark, 1906–76.

Moulton, William F., and Alfred S. Geden. *A Concordance to the Greek New Testament according to the Texts of Westcott and Hort, Tischendorf, and the English Revisers*. 5th edition. Revised by Harold K. Moulton. Edinburgh: T. & T. Clark, 1978.

Nestle, Eberhard, and Kurt Aland (eds.). *Novum Testamentum Graece*. 26th edition. Stuttgart: Deutsche Bibelgesellschaft, 1979.

Rahlfs, Alfred (ed.). *Septuaginta*. New York: American Bible Society, 1935.

Reicke, Bo. *New Testament Era: The World of the Bible from 500 B.C. to A.D. 100*. Translated by David E. Green. Philadelphia: Fortress, 1968.

Rienecker, Fritz. *A Linguistic Key to the Greek New Testament*. Translated and edited by Cleon L. Rogers Jr. Grand Rapids: Zondervan, 1980.

Scholer, David M. *A Basic Bibliographical Guide for New Testament Exegesis*. 2d edition. Grand Rapids: Eerdmans, 1973.

The Septuagint Version of the Old Testament and Apocrypha, with an English Translation. Reprinted Grand Rapids: Zondervan, 1975.

Silva, Moisés. *Biblical Words and Their Meaning: An Introduction to Lexical Semantics*. Grand Rapids: Zondervan, 1983.

Tenney, Merrill C. *New Testament Times*. Grand Rapids: Eerdmans, 1965.

Van Voorst, Robert E. *Building Your New Testament Greek Vocabulary*. Grand Rapids: Eerdmans, 1990.

Vaughan, Curtis (ed.). *The Bible from Twenty-six Translations*. Grand Rapids: Baker, 1988.

Wigram, George V. *The Englishman's Greek Concordance of the New Testament*. Reprinted Grand Rapids: Baker, 1979.

Zerwick, Maximilian. *Biblical Greek Illustrated by Examples*. Translated by Joseph Smith. Rome: Pontifical Biblical Institute, 1963.

Index of Names

Index of Scripture

1. TEN ESSENTIAL Tools - p. 36 -
2. SEVEN ADVANTAGES To COMPARING NT VERSIONS - p. 41 -
3. HelpFul SOFT-WARE PACKAGES - p. 59 -
4. AN OUTLINE FOR EXEGESIS - p. 66 -
5. A QUICK SUMMARY OF GREEK EXEGESIS - p. 92 -